A NEW BEGINNING

Part I

A WWII Historical Fiction Thriller Novel

Emily Higgs

Copyright © 2024 Emily Higgs

All rights reserved. No part of this book may be used or reproduced in any form whatsoever without written permission except in the case of brief quotations in critical articles or reviews.

This book is a work of fiction. Names, characters, businesses, organizations, places, events and incidents either are the product of the author's imagination or are used fictitiously. Any resemblance to actual persons, living or dead, events, or locales is entirely coincidental.

CONTENTS

Chapter 1 5

Chapter 2 11

Chapter 3 18

Chapter 4 31

Chapter 5 43

Chapter 6 53

Chapter 7 62

Chapter 8 75

Chapter 9 87

Chapter 10 97

Chapter 11 106

Chapter 12 116

Chapter 13 130

Chapter 14 140

Chapter 15 151

Author Note..163

About the Author 164

1

Chapter One

4,000 feet above the French landscape in 1941

"This is First Officer Louella Sterling with a transport company of twenty P-51 Mustangs," I radioed to Allied ground control a few miles away, "looking to land on runway 24 in about ten minutes." Leading the formation of British Air Transport Auxiliary pilots, I kept an eye out for other aircraft on the bright horizon. Our job was to fly twenty fighter planes to a covert airstrip in occupied France, where they would be used in action within a few days.

With an all-female crew, I was keen to prove to the officers that we could do more than just mechanic work and fly from London to Cheshire.

"This is Spitfire Runway 24, and you are cleared to land, ma'am. Do I hear an American accent in your voice?"

I grinned slightly and responded, "Yes, sir. I'm a temporary Tory until orders arrive from the States. And you?"

"I am from Connecticut. When the war started, my Yale education did nothing to help me, but I did get a position in intelligence, which was exactly what I had hoped for. I'm glad to hear another American around here."

He gave me the airfield coordinates and signed off, allowing me to convey the orders to the other females in my squadron.

"This is Louella," I stated over the radio, not feeling the need to speak professionally with them because there were only twenty of us. "I just talked to ground control. It's a tiny airport, so landing everyone will take some time. Simply remain in the pattern until it's your turn, then move out of the way quickly. Remember to account for the short distance and soft terrain. I will be the last one in the air."

Muriel Dalton, one of my dearest friends and the only other officer in the group, said, "Are we following the typical order—where Joan goes first?"

"I was thinking you could lead the way," I remarked with a tiny giggle, gazing out my window to my right and seeing her alongside me, "and help everyone when they land." She turned to look at me through the glass and smiled.

"Thank you, Lou. Joan, are you okay with that?"

"Yes, ma'am," she said, "I think I like it better that way." I lowered my flaps ten degrees to slow my plane down, and I could dimly hear the rest of them over the noise of my own engine. These ladies made me so proud, and thinking about how hard they'd worked to be here just made me love them more. They had all completed every criterion with tenacity and elegance, even if their male colleagues were held to half as rigorous standards.

"First Officer Adams," someone cried frantically, "there's a German convoy behind us on the horizon." My stomach sank.

"How many?" Another voice said, "At least twenty-five, perhaps more. They resemble Messerschmitt 109s to me."

With shaky hands, I retracted my flaps from their landing position and armed the cannons, instructing everyone to do the same.

"We are not going to lead them to the airfield," I said firmly, "but that means we cannot outrun them. Everyone—"

"Ma'am?" someone interrupted. "Our firearms aren't functioning. Nobody's is. Are they updated P-51s, or is there a switch we're not aware of?"

My thoughts raced, and I peered out toward Muriel's plane. The firing mechanisms were still intact and functioning properly, but there was no ammo. The Air Transport Auxiliary had provided us with fighter aircraft, but nothing to fight with. On a flight over the Occupied Zone. My heart pounded with rage.

"Alright. Everyone, pull your weapons back in to decrease drag and prepare for evasive manoeuvres." I was silenced by the thunderous sound of an explosion, and the crimson glare of fire behind me projected my shadow on the control panel. My ears rang, and my fingers shook.

A scream pierced my ears through the headset, and I hurriedly whirled around, hoping to get a glimpse of what was going on behind me.
"Millie is going down," someone yelled out, "and they're shooting hard at us."
"Muriel," I replied. "You take the right side, and I'll take the left. We'll split off, and it will be up to each of you to watch out for each other and protect yourselves. Do not prevent radio communications; instead, use them for critical communication. Split. Over."

Bullets flew all around me as I turned hard to the left, gripping the control stick in horror. I had just led these ladies to their deaths. I did a sharp drop, and three Nazi aircraft pursued me, firing incessantly. Pulling up as late as possible, I heard one of them lose control and crash into the ground behind me, but the other two pursued me even more closely. The radio broadcasts were filled with cries and pleas for aid, but without firearms, there was nothing we could do. One by one, I saw the helpless planes crash to the ground, their pilots desperately trying to save the burning aircraft.

"Parachutes!" I yelled at them, surprised that none of them had considered using them.

"There are none, First Officer," someone replied.

"We're all trying." A second later, I heard the connection severed, and an explosion on the ground rocked my lungs. Dead. I touched the back of my own seat and my heart dropped. She was right; the aircraft were not yet equipped for emergency bailouts. We were all sent out as movable targets, with every asset stripped from us. I was outraged with the people in control.

"Muriel, are you still flying?" I grunted, jerking my controls and applying heavy right rudder to shake a Nazi off my tail.

"Barely," a crackling radio transmission stated, "my left wing is on fire and I'm about to stall." If she stalled with a burning wing, she would go into a spin that would be difficult to recover from.

"Just get on the ground, everyone. Please don't—"

"First Officer," someone began saying, "there is—"

The hit resonated throughout my aircraft, and I could feel the scorching heat emanating from the tail. Bullets smashed through the metal, producing piercing shrieking noises that made me want to pull my ears out.

A piece of metal smashed into the back of my skull, and I clenched my teeth in pain. Falling rapidly to the earth, I anxiously tried to change the dial to communicate with the American on the airstrip.

"This is First Officer Louella Sterling," I cried as the plane flipped upside down and my head slammed against the glass above. "We've been attacked. You must aid us."

He attempted to respond, but all I could hear was the humming of a useless engine as we sank downward. I vomited out the last coordinates I could recall, then screamed out as flames engulfed the plane's tail behind me. I was about to roast alive. The aircraft rolled over many times in an uncontrollable spin, with none of my controls responding. Blood smeared the glass above me, and I could feel my seat belts cutting into my stomach.

The nose struck the ground first, slamming the control panel into my legs and chest. Flames erupted from the engine as the plane pitched over and landed upside down. I passed out, covered in blood and dangling from the seat strap around my neck.

2

Chapter Two

Munich, Germany, 1944

"Fräulein Bauer," Albert Reinhart said, approaching my shabby desk in the Munich newsroom. "Have you finished researching for my article yet?"

I replied with a patient grin, "No, sir, I haven't. It should be ready by seven o'clock. I had a little issue obtaining sources since ladies are not permitted in the backrooms and social clubs where your subject spends the majority of his time. And Mr. Huber stole my typewriter again, sir, and the ink ribbons stopped working."

The middle-aged editor lifted his eyebrows. "If you want to keep your job at the *Völkischer Beobachter*, Fräulein, you need to stop making excuses. The Führer needs every Aryan's assistance in this matter. Schnell!"

He moved away and took a seat in his large office across the room, clicking away with a pen while his feet were up on the desk. Fuming, I wiped the perspiration from my brow and resumed working on the damaged typewriter. The metal folding chair I'd dragged from the basement was too short for the desk I recovered from the alleyway, so I had to squat on my knees to peer inside the machine.

I persuaded myself, "Just a little longer here, and you'll be back in America."

The Office of Strategic Services engaged me to infiltrate German media and propaganda centers because I spoke German well and had the Aryan complexion that every American and British spy desired. Of course, I wasn't Lina Bauer; my true name was Louella Sterling. My husband, Bennett, was the OSS's Major General and Information Coordinator. We collaborated on many tasks.

Most of the time, I would post coded advertising and secret messages for the Resistance troops and gather any information I could discover, but lately, I was simply trying to stay quiet as bombs ravaged the city from above. By the end of the day, I had repaired the typewriter, persuaded a seventeen-year-old lad to go into the hotel nightclub and ask my target of interest a few questions, and wrote six pages of material on him.

After reapplying lipstick and running my fingers through my dark blonde locks, I took a deep breath and entered the editor's office with his information.

"Here it is, sir," I said as gently as possible, "everything you asked for."

He moaned and stroked the bald patches on the sides of his head, flicking through it slowly. As I was about to depart, he said, "Warte ab." I paused and turned to face him again, worry swelling in my chest. He never wanted me to stay in his office longer than necessary.

"Yes, sir?"

"I've noticed you've been getting a lot of telegrams lately. It seems to be distracting you from the responsibilities assigned to you."

My mouth became dry. "I apologize, sir. I will do better, I promise. I appreciate your understanding." To escape further questions, I swiftly turned toward the door and started to rush out of the room.

"Halt, Fräulein," he yelled, with conviction in his eyes. "Sit down." I cautiously perched on the edge of one of his chairs, clutching my shivering hands in my lap.

"If it had been my choice," he said, "you would never have entered this building. You lack sturdiness and depth in your work, and your lack of inventiveness is a disgrace to our office, which serves the Führer. You can't comprehend the news as well as the men here, and you're weak and stupid. Fräulein Bauer, your sole task should be to produce future state servants."

I was astonished. I took a deep breath and started to speak, but he interrupted me.

"Let me see your telegrams."

"They are nothing, sir. Just messages from my family in Berlin."

"So, it should be no issue for me to view them, right? If I discover that you have a hidden lover, Fräulein Bauer, you will be terminated immediately. There should be no women in this workplace, especially married and preoccupied ones."

My heart raced. They were well-coded, and I wasn't concerned about his deciphering them, but the suspicion worried me. If he believed anything was wrong with me after reading them, he'd dispatch the secret police to murder me without hesitation. I quietly took the telegrams from my desk and returned them to his office, handing them off casually.

Reinhart carefully looked through each one and laid them down in irritation when he was done, glancing up at me to assess my reaction. I remained calm.

"Go home, Lina Bauer. And report back tomorrow morning with details on the Führer's four-year plans. It better be a step above this junk," he said, brandishing my day's work and dropping it into the garbage can, "or you'll be fired. You may already be, Bauer, depending on what *schiesse* you compose tonight."

Running through the packed streets of Munich with my head down, I made my way to Frau Weber's home, the only place I knew of where I might borrow a functional teletype machine.

Frau Weber, a devout Nazi Party member, gave me complete access to her radio teletype. I explained to her that I had distant relatives in America who were attempting to relocate to the Führer's new Germany, and she was seldom home to keep an eye on me.

The OSS in Washington, D.C. had the means and people to send telegraph communications to me via New York, England, France, Berlin, and eventually Munich, but I did not. Despite its impracticality, I had to use the teletype to contact someone in the United States on rare occasions in order to avoid the Nazi authorities intercepting my communications.

I knew I needed to get out of Munich before Herr Reinhart investigated further and sent the secret police after me, but it was up to the OSS to send a plane for me. I placed my things on Frau Weber's sofa and switched on the massive apparatus, causing it to whirr loudly. I called the remote number for the OSS office's teletype machine and began working as rapidly as possible. There was no point in fully encoding or attempting to make it flow like a normal letter; it would go straight to the United States.

"Hello, cousin Simon. I hope the family is doing well. Perhaps I will pay a visit soon. In three days, I'll be in Starnberg, hoping to visit pals. Things are going well at work, but I'm bored of interviews."

I hesitated, my fingers hovering above the primitive keyboard.

"I love you."

As I composed the message, an anxious intern in that musty office with those green chairs called Major General Sterling to read the letter addressed to one of his code names. The family mentioned the OSS, and my desire to see them was more of a plea than a straightforward declaration.

The comment about Starnberg was to inform them that I would be ready for a plane to pick me up in three days, and that in order to determine which secret airfield to land on, they would use a map to identify whichever city was 50 miles west of the one I named. It was a straightforward operation, but it would be almost impossible to understand if the remainder of my letter was intercepted.

My phrase about work informed them that I hadn't been discovered yet, but people were becoming suspicious and asking questions about me. Just then, a door slammed behind me, and Frau Weber walked in with her hands full of groceries. I snatched the paper from the machine and placed it into the pocket of my dress before swiftly turning it off.

"Heil."

"Heil."

"Another letter?" she remarked coolly, accepting my help with the food as we carried it into her small kitchen. I nodded.

"Yes, madam. My relatives are yearning to escape the American cesspool.

Thank you for allowing me to use your machine."

She waved dismissively and patted me on the shoulder as I approached the door, saying, "It's nothing, my darling. Anytime. *Auf Wiedersehen*."

I waved at her on my way out and groaned as I ran upstairs to my flat, clutching the crumpled paper in my hand.

3

Chapter Three

Once entering my flat, I put my belongings on the filthy couch and removed my cap. Of course, I had to leave my flat after paying the rent this month, I reasoned with a slight grin. I switched on the government-issue radio on my desk and started making soup with the remaining vegetable supplies. If I left Munich the following night, I could take the train to the concealed airport at Herrsching, which was 50 miles west of Starnberg.

There would be no hurry; I was certain that Herr Reinhart had not pieced anything together other than the fact that he did not want me in his propaganda office. After eating supper and wrapping up the remaining soup to last me a few days without ration cards, I lumbered into my little bedroom and started laying out my nightgown. I froze. The bogus identity documents buried under the mattress were poking out a bit, and my bed was much cleaner than when I left it that morning. Someone was here. I thought I needed to fetch my gun.

As I began to turn towards the door, a large arm curled around my neck and choked me. I gasped for air and planted my feet firmly before reaching back and elbowing my assailant in the face. He let me go for a moment, giving me time to gather my thoughts before the next onslaught. There were three Gestapo officers in my room, one with a pistol and the other wielding a knife. The man I had struck was slowly getting to his feet, wrath in his eyes. They all appeared to expect me to swoon or weep at the sight of them, but I was not going down without a fight.

"Louella Sterling," one of them started to say, "you are under arrest—" I knocked the revolver out of his grasp and pushed him into my wardrobe with the sole of my foot, burying my dark red heel into his stomach. He stumbled away, in agony. With my back to the soldier next to him, I dragged him to the ground and slid away, knocking the last man off his feet with my knees.

As one of them reached for the pistol, I kicked it away and ran at him, striking him hard in the face, taking a few blows in return. Just as I knocked him unconscious, another grabbed my hair, dragging me to the ground, and stomped on my hand as I attempted to break his hold. My mind raced with a million thoughts.

He put his hands around my neck and sank his fingers into my flesh with force. These soldiers, although tough and pain-tolerant, lacked agility and a sense of purpose without their weapons. I groaned and dragged my heel down his shin, causing him to let go of me.

Suddenly, a tremendous pain gripped my stomach, and I glanced down to see a knife in my side, coated in blood as one of them removed it. I cried out in agony and dropped to my knees, shocked.

With a frenzied burst of adrenaline, I lunged at the man wielding the knife, gouging his eyes with my thumbs. The final Gestapo officer slammed me against the wall and punched me repeatedly. I grabbed him by the shoulders and pressed my knee into his crotch, forcing him to lose balance and giving me the edge. He fell unconscious within seconds.

I slumped, blood streaming from my nose and a wound on my side. Gasping for air, I moved to the side of my bed and grabbed my thin white duvet, pressing it against my side to stem the bleeding. Knowing I needed to leave before they came to or additional officers arrived, I started packing a few possessions into a bag. I couldn't breathe, and I had no way of contacting Bennett or anyone from the OSS.

I attempted to stand but screamed in pain as agony radiated throughout my body. "Help," I cried out to no one in particular. "I need help." It quickly became clear that escaping with my injury would be difficult under the circumstances. I pulled myself into the kitchen and rummaged through the drawers, retrieving my pistol, a needle and thread, and a box of matches.

Slumped on my couch, I inserted the needle with shaky hands and burned the end to destroy the germs. I had no choice but to stitch myself up. My dress had a large enough hole cut into it, so I didn't have to remove it entirely, and I was relieved that it was a dark color so I could just throw on a coat and head to the train station.

I groaned in agony during the first few stitches and tried to concentrate on breathing, but after a while, I became so numb that it just felt like a dull ache. The fabric I had dragged from my bed served as a makeshift bandage, and after the procedure was over, I clenched my teeth and stood up. My vision was blurred by black dots as I staggered to the coat rack and put my long black coat over my bleeding burgundy dress. The most important thing was that nobody saw the wound.

I limped towards the door, carrying a small bag containing all of my money, notebooks with codes, a small box of food, my handgun, and a portrait of Bennett. I had to get out of here. After wiping the blood from my nose and smoothing my ruffled hair, I put on a pair of outdated sunglasses and some crimson lipstick. I'd need to blend in well.

I went outside and began hobbling to the train station across town, tears flowing down my face as I gripped my side. I felt like passing out.

"Fühlst du dich gut?" an elderly lady sporting a swastika pin on her collar inquired. "Are you feeling well?" I gave a fake grin and nodded.

"Ja, danke schön. I am just tired. Heil Hitler."

"Sieg Heil, Fräulein." I bit my lip as she walked away, clutching my side as more pain tore through my body. The Munich Deutsche Reichsbahn railway station loomed in front of me, with trains entering and exiting from the vast meadows behind the massive structure. I staggered up to the counter and implored the woman anxiously, "Please, I need a ticket to Herrsching today. Can you please—"

She raised her hand and glanced at me, as if she'd heard the question a thousand times that day.

"The only trains going to Herrsching this week are military. You missed your last chance yesterday afternoon, Miss." My mind whirled. How would I go anywhere? I recalled Veronica Hart, another female OSS agent who was now in Stuttgart directing resistance troops before being transferred back to France.

If I went there, she could keep me alive for three days until the aircraft arrived, giving me enough time to get a ticket to Herrsching later.

"What about Stuttgart?" She shook her head, the little feather on her cap bouncing with each movement. "The only ones in the region are heading to Natzweiler, Fräulein. They're just hauling detainees. The

Jews." Exasperated, I looked her in the eyes and attempted to mask my distress.

"Please. Can't I simply ride that? I will be fine." Her eyes widened, and she shouted, "You cannot be serious, Fräulein! They're going to the camp."

"The camp outside of Stuttgart, correct? I need to get there," I said, desperate to reach Veronica Hart. She sneered and waved me aside, starting to assist the next person in line. Before I walked away, I memorized the number of the Stuttgart train on her page and the time it would arrive at the station. I could feel blood seeping through my bandages, and I knew if I didn't seek treatment right away, I'd die or be killed.

Limping out of the station, I leaned against a section of the wall that had been demolished by American bombs and tried to think: I could get aboard the train with the convicts and attempt to jump off once we were near Stuttgart, or I could quietly sleep in an alley while bleeding to death.

Neither option sounded ideal, but I was more tempted to try contacting Agent Hart; we'd been friends for years, and the Gestapo had a hard time catching the two of us. *The Cipher and Artemis,* I thought, referring to our Gestapo nicknames, had finally reunited. Desperate to reach her, I sneaked behind the massive train station and into the field filled with hundreds of empty and waiting freight trains.

The train headed for Natzweiler was easy to spot since it was the last in line and the most run-down. The lengthy freight train lay unattended, waiting for its captives to be loaded after being marched through the city from Dachau.

The inhabitants of Munich had seen hundreds of parades involving thousands of starved Jews, Poles, and Communists; this would be just another regular transfer, and I was relying on the guards' weariness and indifference to overlook me.

Without this train and the opportunity to meet with Veronica Hart, I would not have survived the three days it would take for the American jet to arrive, much less make it to the runway on time. This reckless, desperate plan was my last hope of escaping captivity. I climbed into one of the final train carriages and curled up in the back, taking my revolver from the bag and placing it by my side just in case.

Once again alone, I drew aside my coat to see blood-soaked bandages. I wished I had become a doctor rather than a pilot, but then I realized that it was my experience in the Royal Air Force and that catastrophic accident that brought me to Bennett, who went on to become the chief of American intelligence.

Almost an hour later, hundreds of thundering footfalls echoed over the war-torn German countryside. I jumped to my feet and squeezed myself against the foul-smelling wooden walls in the corner, praying that the Nazi soldiers would not thoroughly search the vehicles before loading them with inmates.

The door swung open, and I held my finger on the trigger of my pistol, dreading with each passing second. I was about to die.

"Schnell!" someone yelled, forcing emaciated men and women aboard the train with me. One man caught my eye, and I raised my finger to my lips, silently begging him not to say anything. He nodded. The people in front of him followed his example, encircling and protecting me from the other Jews and troops.

"Who are you?" a woman questioned me, brushing up against me as the train compartment became overcrowded.

"I'll tell you when the door is closed," I said quietly, "I'm not going to hurt you; I promise." The door was slammed shut, and people started fighting for positions near the small, barred-up window, hoping to save themselves and their families. These folks looked like skeletons, with no hope of a future in their eyes. Children clung to their parents in dread, and young men fought as bravely as they could to defend their sisters. I couldn't take it.

One adolescent boy beside me said, "Who are you? Why are you here? If you are seeking food, woman, we do not have any. Don't you know what kind of train this is?"

I started to respond, clutching my side in anguish, but I couldn't get the words out. Unable to keep myself up and feeling the loss of blood take its toll, I slumped into the tiny group gathered around me and blacked out.

"Ma'am? Hey, wake up! It'll be all right. Mr. Zeller, there's something wrong with her stomach... it seems she's bleeding."

I felt someone start to peel back my coat, and I opened my eyes to see myself curled in a tight ball on the edge of the train compartment, surrounded by the same few individuals who had been there when I passed out.

"Please," I muttered, returning to my senses and pushed away the hand attempting to expose my wound. I trusted these people, but I didn't want them to take advantage of a wounded girl carrying food in her bag.

"Who sent you?" I looked up at the woman who asked the question, searching for any unpleasant or accusatory expression on her face, but there was none.

"America," I said. "The United States sent me." They were astonished.

"Bitte tu mir nicht weh," I implored. "Please do not hurt me. I am an agent with the Office of Strategic Services, and I am on your side. I'm on my way to Stuttgart and plan to leap off the train as we pass an open area near the city. The Gestapo is after me." One young man crouched at my level, his slender knees cracking on the way down, and stared at me in the dim light.

He said in flawless English, "Are you an American spy?"

Surprised by his use of my first language, I muttered, "I am. Y-you speak English?"

He nodded and added, "I was born in America, and my parents

discovered that the banking industry was better in Germany in the 1920s. It seems to have been the wrong choice. Are you hurt?"

"Yes, but I'm fine. I'll be alright. It's only a cut." He lifted his brows, looking between the misery on my face and the blood seeping through the coat. The rest of the group glanced at us in astonishment as we conversed in English, and I noticed, saying, "Ich entschuldige mich. I apologize. We will communicate in German, I promise."

"Do you know where they're taking us?" a mother implored me seriously, hugging her tiny boy to her bosom.

"Natzweiler. The camp is southwest of Strasbourg." A grumble arose from the group surrounding me, and individuals exchanged worried glances.

"Are you all coming from Dachau?" I inquired, wishing I could ease their anxieties but knowing most of them would be dead by midnight.

"Several of us, ja. Others have just been imprisoned." That explained the absence of prison garments on some of them, as well as the large number of aged men and small children; they hadn't yet been processed for death.

"Were you stabbed?" someone inquired, glancing down at where I was gripping my side with bloodied hands. Biting my lip, I nodded hesitantly; it wasn't my intention to share my whole life story with these people, and I didn't want them to think I was looking for sympathy.

"It's fine, really," I said, "I just need to meet my contact in Stuttgart and—" I scolded myself for disclosing so much and for being insensitive to these folks; they'd never be able to get out of here like I could.

Soon, the exhaustion and lack of fresh air in the train compartment diminished their interest in the stowaway American spy, and I sat motionless against the wall, people crammed on both sides of me, the discomfort worse than the odour.

As we approached Stuttgart, I signalled for John Alton, the man who spoke English, to join me.

"Does anybody here speak English?"

"No, I don't think so. Why?" I peered around the train car, but no one seemed to be paying attention to us.

"I have a little food," I muttered in English, "but not enough to feed the entire train. I don't want to cause a riot or injure anyone. Is there anybody here who actually needs it, and could I give it to them secretly? If you want to take it yourself, I will not blame you; but if it's better for you to give it to someone else, that's fine with me too."

He looked down at my bag and muttered, "I've got someone. It's a seventeen-year-old girl who is quite unwell. I suspect she'll make it through the sorting line and be assigned to hard labour, so she'll need energy once we arrive. Should I give it to her?"

I agreed and gently handed him the wrapped packet of soup, watching as he walked to the other side of the train compartment and returned a few minutes later through the crowd of hundreds of Jews gathered around me. "She wept, Miss. She couldn't stand up but wished she could hug you."

"I wish I could do so as well." A young man approached me from his position by the small window and remarked, "Das ist Stuttgart. We are in the countryside around the city. If you're going to get off, this is the safest moment."

Trembling, I rose to my feet and winced in agony as I pushed my way through the crowd to the entrance.

"If anybody decides to follow me," I advised as I stood near the massive wooden door, "although I don't think it would be wise, please wait at least a few kilometers after I jump so that if one of us is caught, the other still has a chance. This war will be won for you, and please know that the Allies are doing everything they can. Thank you for your kindness, and please don't turn me in, but I understand you must do what you need to protect yourself. May God be with all of you."

Holding my silenced pistol in my left hand, I extended my arm through the barred window and gently shot the padlock on the outside of the door, shaking the door until it came loose. I pulled the door open and clung to the sides as the wind blasted through the train cabin. The fresh air appeared to have rejuvenated everyone on the train, including myself.

"If I'm shot," I told John Alton in English, "make sure everyone in this carriage is safe. I don't want anybody punished because of my actions. Okay?"

"Okay, Miss. Adieu."

Holding my bag to my chest like a shield, I leaped off the train and rolled across the field alongside the tracks, stifling cries of anguish as I hit the firmly packed soil. Now all I had to do was wait for the bullets when the soldiers realized someone had jumped from their train. With dirt in my teeth and long grass tangled in my hair, I held the ground like a friend, willing it to hide me.

My whole body trembled as the wheels of the train rushed over the tracks, only a few steps from where I was lying. Hitler's proudest treasure, his railroads, had just spared one enemy spy while taking the lives of so many others. The soldiers stationed on the end of the caboose passed directly over me, oblivious to the runaway agent who had jumped from their train. I could feel their guns fixed on me, ready to blow my head off and seize the codebooks in my bag.

But they passed, and the train became nothing more than a distant rumbling, taking its victims far away from me. I turned onto my back and cried in anguish as blood began to seep slowly from the incision. I drew aside the coat to see blood-caked bandages. The sutures had ruptured in the fall, and the cut was wide open once again. My ribs felt fractured.

I gritted my teeth and got to my knees, taking a few deep breaths before getting up. I had just jumped off a train, I thought to myself. I couldn't wait to tell Bennett.

4

Chapter Four

It took me about an hour to get to the city limits from the rural trains, and my side had been bleeding since I started walking. If I didn't get to Veronica's home soon, I'd die. The city of Stuttgart had been devastated by British and American air strikes. Every street I passed was filled with blackened apartment buildings and collapsing masonry, and people milled about as if nothing had occurred.

If only they realized how fortunate they were compared to the Jews going through the fringes of their city. When I arrived at Veronica Hart's filthy apartment, I leaned against the doorframe and anxiously pounded.

Nobody came to the door for a long time, and my heart started racing. I knocked again, and someone inside responded in a barely audible whisper, "Who's there?"

I raced through my brain for one of my codenames that she'd recognize and hadn't been compromised.

"Agathe Schneider." There was a slight commotion inside, and I could hear her limping to the door with caution. Her prosthetic leg could be heard dragging on the dusty wooden floor.

"Ginny?" I said quietly, adopting her nickname. "It's Cipher." She flung open the door and dragged me inside, glancing behind me to ensure no one saw us.

"Hey, Dutch!" she said quietly, leading me into her flat. "I thought you were dead!"

"I feel like it. I'm sorry to come here," I gasped, "but I had nowhere else to go. Is it safe to speak English here?" She helped me lie down and nodded, adding in English, "Don't apologize. You're hurt badly." She gasped as she pulled down my coat and clothes, revealing my neglected wound.

"Are the spy hunters after you?" she said quietly, grabbing for the blanket to cover me as I trembled. I nodded.

"My boss at the newspaper didn't like having a girl on staff, so he started—" I took a deep breath as she started applying water to the wound, "—

looking for a reason to fire me. He didn't find anything solid, but once the Gestapo was on the case, they pieced it together pretty quickly. I'm quite certain they don't know I'm in Stuttgart."

She smiled as she stroked a few strands of hair off my forehead, sensing my remorse for endangering her.

"Stop worrying. You did the right thing, Louella. I'm thirty-seven years old with one leg… let them try to come after you without getting through me. Have you seen the papers?" I wrinkled my brow, and she walked to the kitchen, returning with the same newspaper I used to write for. An old picture of myself was at the bottom of the first page.

The Gestapo uncovered enemy spy and fighter pilot Louella Sterling, also known as Lina Bauer, the Cipher of the Allies, or Margot Girard, in Munich. After a bloody confrontation with German forces, she managed to escape by using savage methods, killing two officers. Nazi authorities say she has a knife wound on her right side. She is considered armed and dangerous, and it is best to kill her on sight. Any information on Sterling's location should be reported to the closest Nazi Party headquarters.

I raised my eyebrows at Veronica.

"Brutal tactics?" she said, laughing. I laughed and responded, "I gouged one man's eyes out. Self-defence, of course, but I admit that it was a little exhilarating."

"Louella!" she shouted, jokingly striking my arm and getting up. "Well, I suppose that if that's the case, you'll need a bit of a disguise, hmm? Didn't Major General Sterling always say he liked you with brown hair?"

I startled as she flung a bottle of hair dye at me, crying with a grin, "Brown again? Why couldn't the OSS pay for some gorgeous red locks for me sometime? I'm tired of brown hair! But I suppose it'll do. Thank you, Ginny."

"Now," she continued, bringing up a chair next to me, "before we talk beauty, let us work on this wound you've got here, shall we?" I unbuttoned my dress as far as it would go and yanked it back with trembling hands, gasping in agony as the bleeding cloth peeled away from my flesh.

"This is bad, Dutch."

"I know. Can you stitch it up?"

Veronica glanced at me with wide eyes and said, "No, Louella! I can't—"

"I'll talk you through it. It's easy—just like mending a dress. Please; I can't do it myself." After some coaxing, she consented to perform as much of it as she could, but she was clearly not happy about it.

"You're just going to need a needle and thread," I remarked with a sigh, "bandages of some sort, a match, and vinegar or wine or something."

She sprang up and raced about her apartment, gathering all of the supplies and a few extras she considered essential. I sat back, closed my eyes, and tried to breathe to distract myself from the discomfort. She returned with a threaded needle and an unopened bottle of wine in her hand, placing a soiled blanket underneath me to keep the blood off the sofa.

"What do I do? Do you want to drink this?" I smiled slightly and accepted the bottle from her.

"Of course not! Get ready to stitch me up," I replied fiercely as I opened the alcohol and poured it all over my stomach, screaming out in pain as the chemicals cleansed the wound. Veronica grasped my hand and attempted to calm me.

"Okay," I said. "Stitch it up. You can do it, Veronica. Just ignore the blood and make the stitches tight, like we learned in Washington." She sneered and held the needle like it was poison.

"Those medical training classes were a joke, and you know it, Lou." Veronica was right. It was near the start of the war when women were allowed to join the OSS as anything more than secretaries, and they didn't care much about properly educating us, figuring we'd never travel abroad. But here we were.

"It doesn't have to be great, Ginny; just good enough that I can survive until tomorrow." She hesitantly started sewing, and I grasped one of the covers tightly. I was in and out of consciousness the whole time, waking up for a few seconds in agonizing pain before falling out again. I was starting to feel the effects of the blood loss.

Weakness started to take over my body, and I fell into a deep slumber while shivering violently.

I awoke to solitude and serenity, with bandages snugly wrapped around my stomach.

"Veronica?" She raced in from the kitchen on her good leg, holding a massive rifle in her hands and smiling widely.

"You're awake, thank goodness! I thought I'd killed you!" I smiled softly and croaked, "Why do you have that gun? Do you have an assignment from D.C.?" She shook her head.

"Just cleaning it before my trip back into France. I dyed your hair for you; I hope that's alright, darling."

"Of course," I said, "if you think it looks good, I trust you. You're like my big sister."

She burst out laughing and said, "I'm practically old enough to be your mother, Dutch, so I'll take that as a compliment."

Sitting in the chair next to the sofa I was lying on, she said, "I'm worried for you, Louella. The Luftwaffe appears to be shooting down more Allied planes than ever, and I fear that the plane coming to pick you up will not make it, or you'll be shot down on your way to America." I pursed my lips and groaned.

"It's quite possible. I don't even know if they received my message." After a moment's reflection, I said, "I miss Ben, Veronica. I wish this wasn't how things had to be. Of course, I like spying, and working with individuals like you makes it worthwhile, but it's so difficult, you know? I haven't seen my husband in eight months, and being a spy is really lonely."

She hugged me and giggled a bit before bringing her wooden leg up into the chair with her.

"I understand. I understand, Lou. You are aware that you have done an excellent job, right? Twenty-five years old and deemed so dangerous to the enemy that Hitler's top troops are pursuing you? The Cipher conceals her troubles skillfully." I grinned as I ran my fingers over my freshly colored brown hair.

"Thank you, I suppose. I'm just ready to get back to America and figure things out from there. Don't you ever long to go home?"

"All the time," she replied earnestly, entering the kitchen to prepare a meal for the two of us, "but I have nothing to lose here, unlike you. I've got no husband to come back to, no other military job to fall on like you. I'm a civilian, Louella. A lonely civilian with nothing in my life but intelligence work. I've found, dear girl, that spying will be the thing that keeps me alive and simultaneously kills me."

That night, I left Veronica's apartment with an emotional farewell, excessively thanking her for putting herself at risk to help me.

"Nonsense, Dutch," she said with a dismissive hand wave. "I'm delighted you arrived. Take care of yourself and your bandages, would you? If things don't go well in Herrsching, come back here and we'll work out a plan. Please do not get caught." Veronica smirked as she slipped a little box of revolver ammunition into my bag. "In case gouging their eyes out doesn't work." I smiled and embraced her one more time before putting on my cap and racing down the hallway and out of her apartment building.

I took a deep breath to calm myself while wearing one of Veronica's dark grey skirts with a white collar and an even darker grey suit coat over it. I was scared of the spy hunters. I traveled until dusk, hoping to avoid arousing attention while I made my way to the train station across town. Now that everyone knew about the gash on my side, I'd have to be extra cautious not to limp or give myself away, even though I was in tremendous agony.

The Hauptbahnhof train station was a massive structure, with gigantic Nazi flags hanging over each window and posters decorating the outside of the entrance. I shivered at how many troops may be there, waiting for the renowned Louella Sterling to walk through the doors.

"Ein ticket?" the elderly lady at the desk said dryly. I nodded.

"Ja. Zu Herrsching, bitte. To Herrsching." She stamped a little piece of paper and gave it to me with no more words.

In exchange, I placed the money in her outstretched hand and thanked her. While I waited on the platform for the train, the man next to me appeared to be constantly conversing.

"Dannstemming, huh?" he asked me unexpectedly. I startled slightly and wrinkled my brows.

"Was haben Sie gesagt? What did you say?"

"The song, Fräulein. The Ballroom Jive. That's what they're playing on the radio over there. Do you know it?"

Surprised, I shook my head. "I don't listen to much music. It sounds nice, I suppose." He did not stop.

"Where are you from? Why are you going to Herrsching?" I frowned at him and lowered my hat, saying curtly,

"I'm from Augsburg. I'm just visiting family today."

"I am attending the Reichsfinanzschule Herrsching. The finance school there. I'm going to work for the Führer soon."

I faked a grin as the train roared into the station, and I rushed to board before he did. Keeping my head down, I gave the conductor my ticket and entered the car. Soldiers were everywhere, spread across the benches and talking loudly to their pals. My heart sank. I sat as far away from them as possible, thinking about the codebooks in my luggage. In a normal circumstance, I would never have thought to store them in such an obvious location, but I had nowhere else to conceal them. If one of these troops discovered them or identified me, most of the OSS's intelligence work would be lost. How could I have been so careless?

A young mother sat next to me, holding a toddler in her arms and repeatedly apologized for his wailing. I waved my hand.

"Please, Ma'am," I comforted her, "I don't mind. He's adorable."

I was relieved that it was her rather than a soldier or a curious man. She smiled, fatigue visible in her eyes. This woman seemed to have had many restless nights due to air raids. The four-hour overnight train trip was excruciating for me, with every movement or rumble of the engine cutting into my wound. I maintained a straight expression.

Beatrix, the woman next to me, did not urge conversation but was quite kind. I volunteered to hold her child, Karl, while she slept, and she gladly agreed. Holding the seven-month-old infant to my chest, I watched the German landscape pass by at lightning speed. I thought I was nearly home. Bennett. Please wait for me. Please.

We arrived in Herrsching before daybreak, the train's fourth stop on its way to Munich, and I bid farewell to Beatrix and Karl, picking up my tiny suitcase with a fake smile. On my way out of the train station, the man keen on making conversation cried out, "Auf Wiedersehen, Fräulein! I hope to see you again sometime! Heil Hitler!" I saluted, then swiftly turned around, rolling my eyes.

Herr Giroux, a wealthy member of the German resistance in the city, possessed an estate on the outskirts of town that included a private, concealed airfield. Without him, it would be almost impossible to get Allied spies into Germany.

I knocked on his door frantically as the sun rose. The runway behind his home was completely covered in brush and camouflage.

"Who's there?" a groggy voice said from the other side of the door.

"The Cipher. Do you have any shoes for sale today, sir?" I heard a tiny giggle on the other end, and Herr Giroux opened the door, wrapping me in a massive embrace.

"Louella, my friend," he began, bringing me inside. "I didn't expect a visit from you today. They're looking all over for you."

Grinning at the large man's long nightshirt, I sat down in one of the soft seats and fell back, exhausted, gripping my side.

"The OSS should be coming sometime today to pick me up. Have you not heard from them?"

He shook his head and started preparing two cups of coffee with his provisions.

"Nein, I have not heard anything from America in a long time."

"Hmmm," I replied gently, "I do hope they come."

Herr Giroux presented me with a little cup of tea and said, "Would you like to listen to my S-phone system, Frau Sterling? The British government gave it to me; perhaps you'll hear from them. Once I get you set up with the machine, I'll go uncover the runway just in case they come unexpectedly."

I thanked him and followed him to the third level, where I saw him open a closet in one of the rooms and remove a fake oak back. He removed the illegal S-phone from the secret shelf, placed it on the floor in front of me, and adjusted it to the proper settings.

"If any aircraft messages from your American pals arrive, you will be the first and only one to hear them. This is the 'Ground' set, Fräulein, and it is only compatible with aircraft that have the matching 'Air' set. Are you OK?"

"Ja, danke, Herr Giroux." I sat by the S-phone all morning, waiting for a coded signal, but nothing came through. Soon, exhaustion set in, and I fell asleep on the musty wooden floor, cradling the fifteen-pound transceiver to my chest.

5

Chapter Five

"Easy Tare three-five-seven, do you read me?" I awoke to the sound of a radio call and held out the S-phone, hoping to see if I had dreamt it. The grandfather clock in the corner read three o'clock in the afternoon.

"Easy Tare three-five-seven?" A New York accent. I pressed the button, ecstatic, and said, "This is Peter Fox 280. I hear you loud and clear."

"Herr Giroux! I hear them!" I screamed, rushing to the door and yelling down the stairs to where he stood.

The guy on the other end of the radio said, "Peter Fox, I'm with the Air Force 109th Division, and I'm here to pick you up. Charlie Fox sent me."

I grinned. That was Bennett. Thank you.

"What is your position?"

"Turning downwind to runway 2-4. Is the runway clear?"

"Affirmative, soldier, I'll be out there in a minute," I said, hearing the engine hum over the house.

"What type of aircraft are you in?"

"The P-51 Mustang, Ma'am." I raised my eyebrow in astonishment and smiled. I knew that aircraft like the back of my hand, but Women Air Force Service Pilots didn't have as many opportunities to fly it as men did. The prospect of flying in it again was exciting.

"I'll meet you out there," I murmured gently, rising up and carrying the massive S-phone in my hands, the canvas strap tugging around my neck as I went down the steps. While setting the machine on the table and taking up my suitcase from the shelf by the entrance, I noticed Herr Giroux's shoes, indicating that he had not gone outside to inspect the runway.

As hesitant as I was to rouse the elderly man from his nap, I didn't want to leave without informing him.

"Herr Giroux," I said, "I am on my way out the door. Thank you very much for your hospitality." I started walking down the long hallway towards the bedrooms, but something in the kitchen caught my attention, and I did a double take. He had died. Herr Giroux's lifeless body clutched at three terrible knife wounds in his belly while lying on the floor, blood all over his fancy kitchen. I screamed. Stumbling back from the horrific sight, I searched for the killer and groped for the revolver in my backpack, breathing heavily.

Outside, I could hear a P-51 Mustang scream down the runway. I had accidentally guided the pilot into a trap that had already killed Herr Giroux. Trembling in terror and gripping my handgun, I dashed out the back door toward the runway when a gunshot went off. I ducked and dropped the backpack containing all of my possessions. Memories of being shot down in my aircraft filled my mind, and I felt as if I were back in the French countryside, with other women in my detachment crying over the radios and blood splattering over my window as I was flung about the cockpit. It had been a massacre, and I was lucky to escape with my life. I cannot do this again. The man who fired at me wore a white shirt with suspenders and a Nazi insignia on his cap.

I believed him to be a professional spy-hunter, but the fact that he seemed to have targeted Herr Giroux and then left without even going upstairs made me question whether he knew he had just discovered the Cipher of the Allies. The American man had opened the plane's canopy at the end of the runway, prepared to exit and assist me.

"Stay!" I yelled to him, trying to aim at the assailant, "Get the plane ready for me!" I couldn't leave the S-phone transceiver in the house for the Nazis to steal; they'd have access to every Allied signal that attempted to reach them. Running back inside the house, I grabbed the S-phone and smashed it on the stairs, tears flowing down my cheeks at the sight of Herr Giroux's lifeless eyes staring directly at me.

The spy hunter charged into the room, guns blazing, and I dived for cover in the kitchen. My legs slipped over the blood-soaked linoleum as I frantically groped for one of the knives in the drawers. The pilot outside probably thought I had gone mad. As the spy hunter chased me into the house, a gunshot cracked into the wall inches from my head, his eyes glinting with the thrill of capturing the American spy. I felt a bullet graze my neck and shatter the mirror behind me, so I fired blindly at the assailant, blood in my eyes.

He slumped back after being shot in the stomach, and I took advantage of the moment to make my way to the back door. Stumbling out the door, I grabbed Herr Giroux's emergency bag, which contained his false identity documents, photos of loved ones, codes and runway information—anything he knew would be useful if he needed to flee quickly. I lamented that it was too late. I dashed towards the aircraft, baggage in both hands. The name *Geraldine* was painted on the plane's side in yellow and white lettering, as if it were a carnival ride.

"Come on, Mrs. Sterling," the American soldier said, helping me climb onto the wing and leap into the cramped backseat. Pulling up my skirt so I could move more freely, I grabbed his hand and cautiously climbed into the leather seat right behind him, my flight control panel between us. He tried to turn around in his seat to assist me, but I yelled out, "Just go! Get us off the ground. I'm fine." I reached for my headset so we could communicate over the noise of the engine, then belted into my seat as we began accelerating down the runway.

Blood streamed from my neck, and it seemed as if I had ruptured the stitches in my side again, but all I could think of was Herr Giroux. He had died, but I hadn't. I felt responsible. I leaned back and studied the control panel in front of me, hoping not to pass out. When we were safely in the air, the pilot turned back to face me and said, "My name is Captain Chester Dudley. What just happened?"

"Spy-hunter," I gasped. "I'm sorry; I put you in danger without knowing it."

He took something from behind his seat and handed it back to me while steering the plane with the control stick. It was a fine leather jacket with the American flag sewn along the side and the name *Sterling* on the breast. It was Bennett's.

"He told me to bring it in case you didn't believe I was sent by the OSS, but given the circumstances, you cooperated admirably, Ma'am. Use this to stop the bleeding." I grinned slightly, imagining what Ben might say if I returned his blood-stained jacket.

"Oh, come on, Lou!" he would exclaim. "That was expensive." We'd both know he hadn't paid a thing for it, and the OSS would send him another within a few days. Trying to calm my excitement and panic, I took deep, gasping breaths. I was sweating profusely, yet my teeth were chattering.

"Ma'am," Captain Dudley said over the headsets, "we're going to pick up considerable speed in the next five minutes. If you feel the need to pass out, make sure your head is secure so you don't hit the window." I giggled a little at his concern about having a woman on the aircraft.

"I think I'll be quite alright," I answered weakly. "I'm a Mustang pilot as well, Captain."

He stared at me incredulously and asked, "You can fly?" I nodded slightly as I pressed Bennett's jacket sleeve to my neck and held the broken stitches in my side with my other hand.

"That's incredible. Are you doing okay, Ma'am?"

"Don't worry about me," I said above the roar of the Rolls-Royce engine. "Just get us out of Germany."

In reality, I was fairly confident I was going into shock and that if we hit 437 mph, the pressure and G-forces would cause me to lose consciousness.

"Is the Resistance member who owned the runway we just left okay?" he quietly asked. "I usually hear him over the radio." The thought of Herr Giroux's body lying on the floor brought tears to my eyes. I could have saved him if I hadn't been so concerned with myself.

"He's dead."

"I'm sorry. It's my fault, isn't it?" he replied sadly. "That Nazi wouldn't have come unless he saw my plane. I'm really sorry, Mrs. Sterling." I attempted to respond, but a wave of nausea hit me, and I gasped for air as pain surged through my body. More blood poured from the wound on my neck, and I started to fear I'd bleed to death before we reached England.

"Ma'am?" he stammered as he turned around to see me much more covered in blood than before. "You need to go to a hospital. I'm going to take us—"

"No," I cried, seizing my control stick and correcting the spin and descent he was about to initiate. "I'm fine. You are not landing on enemy territory, Captain; I won't allow it." He turned and looked at me incredulously.

"Mrs. Sterling, you'll die if you don't get medical care. I'll just pull her down, and then—"

"And then what?" I said, my hands trembling violently as I pressed the leather jacket to my neck. "The Nazis don't have very good hospitals in their extermination camps, sir. Just keep going. Please, I insist." Captain Dudley groaned.

"Are you like this with your husband as well?" I couldn't help but grin and respond, "I guess. Is it bothering you, sir?"

"Ma'am, I'm not used to females taking the controls from me. But then again," he added, "you're officially my copilot, so you have every right. Major General Sterling will kill me."

I took a deep breath and adjusted my seat belts, slouching down and trying to manage the pain coursing through my body.

"He won't kill you; he'll just tell you to do whatever I say. And I'm telling you to keep going and forget I'm even back here, Captain." He groaned but obeyed me, staying silent while cautiously checking on me every few minutes. I was uncomfortable and in more pain than I had ever been when my adrenaline wore off, but I stayed quiet. Just as we approached the German border, I heard a loud rumble behind us and turned around to see a Nazi fighter pursuing us closely.

"Captain," I said firmly, "you've got a Messerschmitt 109 on your six." He grumbled under his breath before flipping a button on his control panel, generating a slight buzzing sound underneath us. He was firing the guns.

"Do you have a plan?" I asked as we accelerated, the other aircraft closing in.

"Not really, Ma'am," he said tersely. "I've never done anything like this before. My job's been more transportation and admin." Wonderful, I thought to myself, we're both going to die.

"Do you know the inverted vertical reverse maneuver, Captain?" I asked, gripping my side in pain as he tried to shake the German with a quick right turn. He looked at me with startled amazement.

"We can't do that, Ma'am. I've heard of it, but I don't know how."

"I do. If you handle the guns, I'll take the control stick and rudder pedals." I wasn't sure if I could execute the move in my current state, but this high-ranking commander wasn't much help in the middle of a dogfight. Bennett would die if he knew what I was about to attempt.

"Alright," he said, "Oxygen masks. Then it's your plane, Ma'am." I fastened the bulky mask to my face and grabbed the control stick from the seat between my knees. All around us, German rockets whizzed past the glass. I was desperate to get out of his reach and in front of him. I took a deep breath and said a quick prayer before pulling the control stick into my belly as far and swiftly as I could. Captain Dudley and I were brutally pushed back into our seats as we climbed rapidly, and I cried out in pain as blood splattered on the glass to my right from my neck. The aircraft stalled, and the captain hit his head on the glass above us.

I pressed down on the rudder pedals with both feet. We were now facing the ground beneath us, my free hair streaming down all around me. The propeller alone caused the aircraft to do an almost full 180-degree rotation. We were free-falling for about two thousand feet, with almost no speed, until I moved the control stick forward again, negating the maneuver. Captain Dudley stared back at me in astonishment as we found ourselves behind the enemy at a much lower altitude. We had disappeared from the German's line of sight.

"Shoot!" I cried into the headset barely hanging onto my head, shaking violently from the G-forces and sheer panic. "It's your plane now. Just shoot him and get us out of here!" He pushed us forward in pursuit, firing continuously at the aircraft in front of us, and smoke began to pour from its tail. The Messerschmitt was crashing to the ground, and I watched as the pilot bailed out of the burning aircraft.

"Let's get out of here," the captain said, turning back to our heading and removing his oxygen mask. I did the same, leaning over the edge of my seat to throw up. The pressure change from the dive seemed to have been too much for my body. When we were certain the threat was gone and the Pyrenees mountains were visible in the distance, Dudley Chester raised his eyebrows at me.

"I've never seen anything like that in my life, Ma'am. I'm impressed."

"Thank you," I replied faintly, placing a hand on my stomach as if in a fog. "I think I'm bleeding."

"I know, Mrs. Sterling."

6

Chapter Six

"Mrs. Sterling? It's okay; it was just a dream. Are you okay?"

I groggily opened my eyes to see Captain Dudley looking back at me from his seat, concerned. The moon in the night sky cast an eerie light across the whole aircraft.

"What's going on?" I asked.

"You cried out in your sleep, Ma'am. I've been trying to rouse you for a few minutes; we're on our way into London now. Apparently, physicians are ready to take you as soon as we arrive, and you will be on your way to New York City."

Looking down, my quivering hands were coated in my own blood, as was the bag containing all of my stuff, which was resting in a tiny pool. I couldn't recall the nightmare, but I had a sense the suffering I felt was genuine.

"How long will I have to stay here in England, Captain?" I muttered and groaned as I moved in my seat.

"I don't know; I suppose that is up to you, m'lady."

I chuckled a bit and said, "Captain, you don't have to treat me like royalty. 'Cipher' is only my pseudonym, I promise you."

"Ma'am, you still outrank me. And I respect what you do more than you realize. Everyone hopes they could have the job you have, but few realize how difficult it is. Mrs. Sterling, spying is an unpleasant profession, but you wear it beautifully. Moreover, you saved my life back there with that Luftwaffe aircraft."

The runway lights could be seen below us, and he softly steered us there with perfect precision.

"Thank you, sir," I answered hesitantly. "That means a lot."

I was in and out of consciousness when Captain Dudley landed the aircraft, and military and medical teams swarmed us like birds, but I gripped Bennett's leather jacket close to my breast.

"Mrs. Sterling," Dudley exclaimed as he dashed behind the stretcher I was being carried on, "I'll be here when you wake up, okay? Can I do anything to—"

"Yes," I said breathlessly. "Contact the OSS. Let them know I'm okay."

He nodded and joined me as far into the operating room as they would allow, standing outside in the waiting area as the stretcher was wheeled into the well-lit room.

"How long have you had this wound?" the doctor said as he ripped away my garments and placed a mask over my nose.

"In four days. This one," I attempted to gesture to my neck, "I received yesterday." I fell asleep before I could hear his answer.

Pain surged down my spine, and I cried out, unable to open my eyes or regain my bearings. I could feel a bandage on my stomach, but my neck felt numb and aching.

"Mrs. Sterling, it's okay. Simply open your eyes gently. You are in London, at St. Bartholomew's Hospital."

A young nurse stood over me, a little grin on her face, and placed a glass of water to my lips. I was in a big hospital corridor separated by curtains, with the sounds of unhappy patients reverberating around the room.

"I need to go home. Will I be allowed to return to America soon?"

"An American Air Force jet is planned to pick you up this evening, ma'am. Is that satisfactory?"

I nodded with a grimace and said, "Wonderful. Thank you. What is your name?"

"Elsie," she said shyly, clearly unaccustomed to her war-torn patients asking such questions.

"That's a great name," I murmured faintly. "Do you know what they did to my injuries? I can't really feel them."

She nodded, and another sufferer behind a curtain cried out in anguish, begging someone frantically.

"Twenty-six stitches in your side and thirty-one on your neck."

I gave a gasp.

"It doesn't seem too awful, ma'am, and it will heal quickly. My fiancé previously had forty in his leg, and the scar is hardly visible today, doll." After a little pause, she said, "Have you a sweetheart waiting at home?"

I smiled, nodded slightly, and said, "I do, really. I miss my hubby tremendously; it's been ten months since I last saw him. He's the epitome of heartache if I've ever seen one." She gave me a sideways look and a little smile when I said how much I adored him.

"Is he a spy as well?" she asked.

I stared up at her in terror. Nobody was supposed to know that I worked in intelligence; I was only a wounded American Air Force pilot on an aircraft transport operation that went wrong.

"Don't worry," she chuckled, "nobody knows but me. Your secret is safe."

"But why do you think—"

"Forgive me, Mrs. Sterling, but most pilots do not sustain knife and gun wounds in an aircraft. And when you were sleeping, you were murmuring German. I don't know many Americans who dream in German, unless they've lived there for a long time. And your last name is Sterling, for goodness' sake! Your husband must be Major General Bennett Sterling, correct?"

I was astonished. "Please don't tell anyone who I am; I can't risk it."

She grinned as she pulled the blanket up over me, muttering, "I won't. Now sleep; you have seven hours till the jet arrives to pick you up and transport you back to that 'hunk of heartache' Major General Sterling."

I awakened to the noises of wretched soldiers all around me, with thin, white curtains as the only thing separating us. Elsie was seated in the corner, a little book on her lap, and she glanced up excitedly as I moved.

"You are awake, Mrs. Sterling! I'm relieved; I was expecting to have to wake you up myself when the aircraft arrived. No offense intended, ma'am, but I wouldn't want to be the one to wake you up from a nightmare."

I laughed. "I quite understand." Bennett's leather jacket was thrown over me, and a rough pen-and-ink depiction of the American flag was tucked under my hand.

"Who did this?" I inquired with a wry grin, unfolding it to examine it.

"All of the nurses helped me get the blood out of the jacket, and one of the soldiers overheard us discussing you. He requested a piece of paper and expressed his gratitude for your help. Apparently, his late wife was also an American."

I fought back tears and slipped the picture into Bennett's coat pocket.

"If you see him," I said, "thank him for me. The generosity you guys have shown me means so much to me. I won't forget it, Elsie."

Soon, I was brought to the London military airport to meet the jet that would take me back home.

Clutching my suitcase in one hand and my painful side in the other, I staggered out of the fancy automobile, surrounded by troops and high-ranking officials. Although my identity was intended to be kept secret, it didn't seem that they were concealing the fact that I was an American with a legitimate cause for being in London. I simply prayed I wasn't jeopardizing anyone.

Soon, the aircraft arrived: a B-17 bomber that had previously halted in the British Isles to provide supplies to the Royal Military. It looked enormous and robust, which was not what I had anticipated for my nonstop journey back to the States. The name *Miss Irish* was painted in green letters on the side, and I was unsure whether I wanted to hear the tale behind it. Two American pilots emerged from the cockpit, wearing wool-lined jackets to combat the frigid conditions in the unpressurized cabin.

"Mrs. Sterling?" one of them said gently, reaching out his hand for me to shake. "It is an honor to finally meet you. I'm First Lieutenant Richard Forester, and this is Second Lieutenant Jack Granger." My eyes expanded slightly, but I kept a straight expression. First Lieutenant Rob Forester was also an OSS officer and served as my communication contact when I was undercover in Munich.

"It's great to meet you both. Do you two work together frequently?" The question was meant for Forester, and I was attempting to figure out whether Lieutenant Granger was aware of our secret identities and the actual reason I was in England.

"Oh, not too much," Forester remarked, clapping his pal on the back and holding out his arm to me. "Granger, will you prepare *Miss Irish* for our trip? I'm going to show Mrs. Sterling where she'll be for the whole voyage." He hurried away, and Forester carefully guided me to the stairway inside the Flying Fortress. I turned to look at him and grinned.

"Agent Radcliffe, huh? Why did they deploy another intelligence officer on an Air Force transport mission? Not that I'm disappointed to see you, but this seems a bit over your pay grade."

He grinned and said, "I am honored, Dutch. Your Major General Sterling requested that I ensure your safe return home, and I'll be returning to France as soon as I drop you off in Jersey."

"How much does Ben know about my condition?" Forester gave me a strange glance. "If you don't mind my asking, what is your current condition? All we know is that you were injured but are doing okay. When I talked with him on the phone earlier, he seemed skeptical of the stories."

I bit my lip as he assisted me into one of the chairs, mumbling, "It's nothing to be concerned about. Stabbed in the stomach and a gunshot clean through my neck"—I pulled aside the collar of Bennett's leather jacket to reveal the bandages—"and I believe I shattered a few ribs leaping off of a train, but they're mending nicely on their own." He looked surprised and began to chuckle before realizing I was serious.

"Buddy-boy will have a heart attack, Dutch. You know how concerned he is about you after what happened in 1941."

I rolled my eyes. "Everyone keeps bringing this up, as if I'm going to forget, Richard. I survived that and this… Whatever this abominable war throws at me, I'll get through it. Exactly like everyone else. I'm not the only one in this battle who has seen something terrifying."

"I understand. Simply keep yourself safe for our sakes. I'll be in the cockpit in case you need anything."

"Thanks. And Richard?"

"M'lady?" He tilted his helmet.

"What else did Ben mention when you talked with him over the phone?"

Lieutenant Forester glanced down sheepishly and chuckled gently. "He thought you'd bring his leather jacket; without it, he feels naked."

7

Chapter Seven

The French landscape, one hour after the aircraft crash in 1941.

"Muriel!" I yelled as I dragged myself across a field smelling of burning lavender and metal. "I'm coming, I promise! Just hold on!" I crept toward the ruins of another airliner, blood running down my face, while holding my shattered ribs with one hand. I'd fallen about a mile distant and spent almost an hour hunting for survivors in other wrecked aircraft. I was close to dying from exhaustion and blood loss, but I couldn't just give up searching. These were my buddies, and I felt responsible for everything.

Muriel's agonizing screams resonated through the blazing flames in the Mustang plane's shell, and I couldn't keep my tears from falling. Survive now, and grieve later. It was pointless. My legs had been crushed by the control panel upon impact, and blood continued to flow from the back of my skull, where I had painfully extracted a piece of shrapnel when the aircraft was struck. Burns flashed over my back.

"Louella," Muriel whispered faintly when I discovered her hand in the twisted debris and crawled over to examine her. "You're bleeding badly." I grinned slightly and muttered, "I'm an American, sweetheart; I'll be okay." For months, we'd joked about my nationality whenever anything went wrong. The thought of that made her smile, which was all I needed.

"I'm stuck," she muttered, frustratedly attempting to lift the piece of wing on top of her.

"Don't tire yourself out," I growled as I pushed it aside and helped her wriggle out from behind it. "We have a long way to—"

I froze. Her legs were a bleeding mess—much worse than mine—and I could see bone protruding through the skin. She became pale at the sight. Muriel's adrenaline appeared to fail her, and all the pain she had previously kept out now flooded back into her consciousness.

"Louella, I can't—"

"Shh," I whispered faintly, cringing as my ribs pained with each breath, "you're going to be fine. I can help carry you while we look for other survivors." She placed a hand on my face and awkwardly wiped blood from trickling into my eyes, a sorrowful expression on her face.

"You can't even walk, Lou; you can't carry me. The Frenchman you spoke to on the radio...does he know what happened?" As I started pulling her away from the blazing remnants of the aircraft, tears flowed down my cheeks, and I panted, "He was American. I told him we were going down, but I didn't get to tell him any coordinates. Who knows how far we are from the airstrip. I've walked almost a mile already."

"And no others?"

"I searched two other planes and found Joan and Edna's bodies. Another plane had exploded and was just a pile of ash. My fault."

She shook her head and grabbed my hand to console me. "You know that's not—" Gunshots rang out all around us, and I covered Muriel with my body, shaking with panic while covering my head with my hands.

"Sie sind Frauen," I heard as the gunfire ceased and footsteps neared. German troops. My heart fell.

"What are they saying?" Muriel said quietly as I drew a sliver of splintered metal between my knees and moved away from her.

"They're surprised that we're women." She gave me a troubled look as a pistol was pushed against my skull.

"Hände hoch," one of the four Nazi troopers said, "Hands up." I obliged, using my legs to hide the hidden piece of metal.

"Du sprichst Deutsch?" I didn't respond. He delivered a powerful backhand, knocking me to my knees.

"Ja," I said grudgingly. My mother spent her whole youth in Austria, and I studied the language extensively as an elective during training. I spoke German almost as well as English.

"Und sie?" one of the men said, waving his rifle at Muriel. "And her?" I shook my head, and Muriel seemed to comprehend what we were discussing.

"I speak Spanish," she said, but the men seemed unimpressed. They were sifting through the debris of her jet, seeking anything useful.

If Nazi forces were already able to locate us, maybe the American working with Resistance intelligence would arrive soon. That was my only hope. Suddenly, the gun shifted from my head to Muriel's, and the soldier cocked it without hesitation. I ran between her and the rifle, yelling, "Nein, nein, bitte!" My unexpected cry halted the man in his tracks, and Muriel gasped, "Louella! That is perhaps the bloodiest American thing I've seen all day. Don't do something foolish just to save me, sweetheart. I'm half-dead anyway."

She smiled slightly, but I couldn't. The realization struck me that she was right. She would probably die before they could register us as POWs. And I'd immediately follow.

"Aufstehen," one of them said.

"He's telling us to—"

"Get up," Muriel grumbled, "I figured. Help me." She recognized the improvised weapon concealed beneath my knees and swept her hands through the debris, bringing a piece of burnt plexiglass near her.

"You take the one on the left," I mumbled, helping her to her feet and allowing her to lean heavily on me. Her legs were soaked in blood, and I observed a nasty incision in her shoulder.

"There're three others, Lou," she said. "Do you plan to take all of them?" I grinned and grasped her hand in pain, the one that wasn't clutching the shard of metal. "Not sure yet."

"Hör auf zu reden!" the man in charge roared, "Stop talking!"

"I'm going to work on getting the guns first," I said. "Go for him after me."

The soldier removed his hand from his pistol and attempted to handcuff me, and I took advantage of the chance.

Lunging for him, I smashed the metal into his neck and kicked the revolver out of his grasp, shouting out in agony with each motion. Muriel had already pulled down the unsuspecting left soldier and was lying on top of his corpse as she attempted to rise up. The bloody glass in her palm shook.

"Nice job," I said, pleased.

I picked up the revolver from the burning grass and fired at the man who was abusing Muriel, striking his forearm. A soldier approached me from behind and placed his arm around my neck, attempting to choke me and pull the weapon from my grasp. The burns on my back sent pain down my spine as I battled to escape, adrenaline doing more harm than good but helping me to forget about the aircraft accident and concentrate on the present issue. I feared becoming a shell-shocked wreck later if I ever got that far.

Muriel shot the man who was attacking her, causing him to drop at her feet as she turned her pistol on me and the Nazi who was holding me.

It was too near. If she attempted to shoot him, it would very likely kill me as well. The soldier recognized this and drew me against him like a human shield, his hands still on my neck. I was about to pass out, but Muriel looked worse than I did.

I wasn't sure what to do. In order to prevent you and your dying buddy from becoming prisoners of war, British female military training did not include hand-to-hand fighting.

"Don't shoot yet," I said, dropping like a heavy weight into the man's arms. He lurched forward, and I reached out to grasp his legs and pull them from beneath him.

"Hündin!" he yelled at me, hitting me square in the face.

"Let me shoot him!" Muriel shouted, staggering forward. I shook my head and let him strike me again, catching his arm as his fist landed on my jaw and dragging him forward to the ground.

Using my momentum, I pulled myself up and elbowed him hard in the back, sliding away enough for Muriel to get a good shot. The bullet made contact. We both collapsed. I fought through my adrenaline immobility and slid over to Muriel, a shocked grin on my face.

"You just did that," I said.

"That was all you."

"That's what every war hero says." She reached up and socked me in the shoulder, and I giggled nervously. We were both in shock, but it was preferable to panic.

"We ought to look for other survivors," I muttered, clutching my ribs in pain. Blood poured down my neck under my white shirt, so I unfastened my black tie to breathe more easily.

"I don't even see any smoke on the horizon, Lou," she said. "They could all be miles away." A deep rumbling emanated from the south as a Jeep produced in the United States started to make its way across the lavender fields.

I rushed up, staggering across the field to get to the vehicle. Two men sat in the front, one older and one in his early twenties, with Rose and Josie sitting in the cargo hold behind them. Their cheeks were smeared with tears, and they both sprang up when they saw me.

"First Officer Adams! You need—"

"Mur—First Officer Dalton is over there," I muttered, losing all consistency in my thoughts. "You have to help her." The young man in the driver's seat sprang out, wearing a dark green sweater over his white collared shirt and heavy-duty military boots. Against my will, I sank in his arms and allowed him to take me into the Jeep. The only thing on my lips was Muriel's name, and I grasped the man's arm as he sat me down and started to leave.

"It's going to be okay, Miss Adams," he mumbled in his soothing American-Irish accent, "I'm going to get Miss Dalton."

"I'm about to pass out," I exhaled, "so you have to promise to treat her first. She's—"

He grasped my hand tightly and nodded. "We will. Mr. Bradford has already called in some more doctors so you'll both be treated. Just rest." The man hurried away after saying something in French to the older man, Mr. Bradford, and I passed out before I could interpret anything.

I groggily opened my eyes, pain coursing through every aspect of my being. The American with the green sweater was so engrossed in his book beside my bed that he didn't notice my pain-induced moan.

"Where's Muriel?" I said, attempting to breathe slowly to alleviate the discomfort in my ribs. He glanced up, surprised, and tucked the book aside.

"She's downstairs, First Officer. Resting just like you are."

"Louella."

"I'm sorry?" He attempted to shift the covers on top of me, but I smacked his hands away. A faint, surprised smile spread over his face, but I couldn't see what was funny.

"I'm not a First Officer anymore. I just killed my entire group." He shook his head and moved the chair closer to me.

"That's not true, ma'am. You have seven other women here that survived because of your forethought to call this station before you crashed, and your clear-headed skill to give them evasive maneuvers that worked."

A sudden flush of rage overtook me, and I grabbed his shirt collar and dragged him down until he was inches from my face, screaming, "We had no guns, sir. None. They sent us on a mission with no guns. And parachutes? How could you have been so thoughtless?"

Every word I spoke felt like fire, but I was too furious to care. Thirteen accomplished, talented women were killed because our bosses did not care about our lives.

"Ma'am," he mumbled, edging away as if frightened I might kill him. "I promise I had nothing to do with that. I think it's despicable, and someone should be held accountable. I—"

"Do you realize what their last moments were like," I yelled at him, "trying desperately to find a way out of the plane as they fell towards the ground? Hearing the screams of their friends dying over the radios? Do you realize what that's done to me, even? I don't expect you to ever care about me, but at least think about the families I'll have to write to! Have you ever had to write to the loved ones of people you were responsible for killing?"

He stared at me with wide, awed eyes. Breathing hard and in severe pain all over, I couldn't stop myself from crying out as it became worse. Getting worked up was the last thing my condition needed, yet the scenario seemed to demand it. In my mind, anyway.

"I'm sorry, Ma'am. I'll, uh, accept full responsibility if you'd like. In the meantime, you ought to get some rest."

I was in too much pain to think of a clever retort. He went to the door and said, "I'll be back in a few hours to check on you, but I doubt you'll be counting down the minutes; please just sleep."

I gazed up at the whitewashed ceiling above me, trying to contain my tears as the reality of what had happened sank in. In my rage, I had failed to gather any information. I didn't inquire where we were, how Muriel was doing, who the other survivors were, what the guys in England were saying, or what my own injuries were.

I lay quietly in the little, flowered wallpaper-covered room for hours, attempting to keep my heart and mind from racing with unwelcome thoughts. It felt like the sounds of explosions and screams would never leave my mind.

I felt bad for shouting at the American. After what felt like an eternity, the door opened and he cautiously walked in again.

"I'm sorry to bother you," he added shyly, "I know you hate me."

"No, actually I—" I stopped myself, wondering what I was about to say. In any case, I refused to back down from the fiery personality I had shown him. He glanced up from the papers he was shuffling on the desk across the room, and the corners of his lips curled into a faint grin.

"Anyway, I just had one question."

I attempted to sit up, but he put up a hand to keep me from becoming tired.

"There were four German bodies where we found you and Miss Dalton," he said, "and I was wondering what happened. Did you kill them?"

I bit my sore lip and glanced down at my hands. "Yes." He lifted his palms to his forehead in surprise and couldn't keep his mouth from falling open. "You and Miss Dalton killed four Nazi officers in your condition? How in heaven's name...how did you do it?"

I couldn't help but smile at his surprise. To be honest, I was surprised myself.

"I don't know," I answered grimly, adjusting my posture slightly. "Desperation, I guess."

He sank in the chair next to the bed and laughed. His hands stretched forward, and he tried to reposition the cushion I was lying against, but I grabbed his arm and trapped it beside me, attempting to conceal my discomfort. I looked him directly in the eyes and asked, "Why do you feel the need to keep touching me? If I need the pillow moved, I'll move it myself."

As I let go of his arm, I observed a look of perplexity in his eyes.

"You're strong. I'm impressed."

"Are you afraid?" He tilted his head, like a puzzled beagle. "I'd never admit it. Yale graduate, remember?"

"Who are the other survivors?" I inquired hesitantly, shifting the topic and taking a deep breath.

He took out a handwritten list from his jeans pocket and gave it to me, relieved not to have to feel embarrassed any longer.

"I can't read it."

"Oh my," he joked. "Is my handwriting that bad?" I gave him a glance. "My eyes can't focus on it."

"For an American, you're not very appreciative of my jokes," he said, "but I can take it. I'll let you rest—"

"No, don't go," I said weakly, collapsing into a coughing fit that made my shattered ribs hurt. With curiosity, he glanced down at my hand clutching his sweater and returned to his seat.

"You're dreadfully obnoxious," I went on, "but you're all the entertainment I have."

He chuckled, reclining back in his chair and resting his feet on the foot of my bed. I did not kick away his feet, feeling little offended by the casual display but happy for the companionship. Mostly because my legs were broken.

"What is your name?"

"Hmm?" The question made him raise his brow.

"Do you have a name...or shall I just call you pretty-boy?"

He smiled. "You think I'm a pretty-boy?"

I rolled my eyes and chastised myself for saying anything. "Not what I meant."

"Bennett Sterling, your humble servant."

8

Chapter Eight

I awakened to low, rumbling turbulence as our B-17 aircraft passed over a woodland. We were in the U.S.

"Doing okay back there?" Forester called from his place in the cockpit.

"Yeah," I murmured, groaning as I got up and moved into my place near one of the weapons, "how much longer?"

He grinned back at me. "Less than 15 minutes before we're on the ground. Sterling is undoubtedly worried sick; we're running a bit late."

I listened closely as Richard and the copilot chatted with the control tower about landing, and I lifted up my shirt to inspect the stab wound that was slowly healing. It still ached to move, but I could tell most of the pain was coming from my shattered rib rather than the gash. Despite the bandages, the sutures on my neck burned like fire. Every movement of my head stretched the gunshot wound, and it took all I had not to cry as I carefully adjusted the bandage.

Looking out the window, I saw the Air Force installation in the distance, and my pulse raced. Bennett was there. During our months apart, the only communication we had was a few quick, coded "I love you" included within intelligence reports. I carried his picture in my backpack wherever I went, but it quickly grew so worn from use that his image was scarcely recognizable. I continued to guard it with my life.

"Will Bennett be at the base when we get there?" I inquired above the sound of the roaring engine.

Richard shrugged. "I haven't heard anything. I suppose we'll know when we're on the ground, hmm?" I raised my brows and took my seat, twisting my matted hair in my fingers and pulling up my coat to cover the unsightly bandages around my neck. If Ben was there, I was going to be ready.

The landing went well, and as soon as we started to taxi off the runway, I collected my belongings and clutched them to my chest.

"In a hurry, Dutch?"

"I've got a date." Forester gently helped me out of the aircraft, and I was instantly swarmed by cameras and reporters. They weren't meant to be there, and no one was supposed to know I was back in the States.

"Mrs. Sterling," someone called as I walked down onto the runway, "the German press has reported your murder at the hands of the Gestapo. Do they truly believe this, or is it propaganda?"

"They have no reason to believe it," I said as loudly as I could, covering my face from the bright lights as I tried to navigate the crowds.

"What were you doing in Europe? Did you conduct any surveillance when visiting our injured soldiers?" I pursed my lips, ignoring the question. They assumed I was there for charitable work, as if espionage were an afterthought.

"Ma'am, could you please tell us what injuries you have right now?"

I ignored it, trying harder to stop hobbling, while another asked, "Does your husband support your spying, or are you going against his will?"

"I fully support her in everything she does," a soft voice murmured, "but I certainly have missed my Cipher girl." My eyes widened, and the crowd had no choice but to part as I collapsed into Bennett's arms, tears of joy and relief flowing down both of our cheeks. Cameras flashed and people yelled all around, but neither of us paid any attention.

"I'm so glad you're alive," he whispered into my hair. "I didn't know what to think after all the reports I've heard."

I placed my hand on his cheek and kissed him with a smile. "I've got some stories to tell."

"You're even more beautiful than I remember, Louella."

"I haven't been to the hairdresser in months, love." He wrapped his arm around me and guided me through the crowd; one swish of his Major General's hat in their direction, and they parted like water.

"I like it. And your brown hair suits you."

Forester ran over to us and shook Ben's hand firmly, smiling at the two of us.

"Looks like you have a following now, Louella," he joked, "but I believe you will handle the celebrity just fine. Regardless of what she says, she will need medical attention. But the British hospital did most of the work." They exchanged glances, and I smirked. "It's not that bad, Bennett."

"You jumped out of a train, for heaven's sake!" Forester exclaimed, "and I'll leave the rest of the stories for you to tell, but you need to rest for a few weeks."

"A train?" Bennett asked, looking at me curiously as he helped me into a maroon Rolls-Royce.

"Later."

Richard Forester hugged me and shook Bennett's hand in farewell.

"Goodbye," he said, smiling. "I'm glad to see you two happy. I have a debriefing in the city tomorrow morning, but I'll be back in Europe by the following evening. I'll return soon."

We said our goodbyes, and he turned to face the press reporters who were chasing him for a statement.

"Gerald," Ben urged the driver, "please take us home and avoid the press wherever you can."

"Yes, Sir. I've been asked to remind you of your meeting with President Roosevelt tomorrow night and to convey the President's wish that Mrs. Sterling attend as well. If you are in good health, Ma'am." I grinned and embraced Gerald Douglas, our dependable driver when Bennett's work necessitated travel.

"I think I'll be quite alright to oblige him," I said. "It has been far too long since I last spoke with him and Eleanor." Bennett's acquaintance with the President had helped him advance to his current position as head of the OSS, and they saw each other as vital partners in the war against Germany.

"How did the press know I was here?" I asked, lying back in my seat, exhausted. "I was quite caught off guard."

Ben shrugged. "I'll phone John Howard later and make sure he speaks with the reporters who were present. They will not publish a single image or sentence without his permission." I rested my weary head on his shoulder and slid my fingers into his grasp.

"I have missed you. I've felt so lonely." He kissed my forehead and said,

"My heart ached for you every time. I went to bed next to an empty pillow. I'm glad you're home."

I dug into my suitcase and pulled out Bennett's leather jacket with a cheeky smile. He gasped, pulled the coat to his chest, and exclaimed, "Oh, thank God! I thought you were gone forever, old friend." I laughed.

"You've got five of these coats, Ben. How could you have really missed this one?"

"Actually, I have six now." Rolling my eyes, I sat back as he said, "They're all different, Louella. This one includes Captain Hale's company patch from before he died, as well as a tear in the sleeve from when I was shot at in Ireland. I have one with the Royal Air Force emblem on it, and it has a convenient pouch on the inside for my rifle. My second one has the OSS patch on it, and it's the one I wore the first time you kissed me."

I pushed him and said, "Of course. How could I ever forget? My commanding officer has never been more enraged in his life!" With a laugh, he ran his fingers through my hair before pausing to notice the bandage poking out from behind my woolen navy-blue coat.

"What's this?"

I gazed up at him and took a long breath, quietly accepting his assurance that he wouldn't go insane if he heard everything.

"Just a small gunshot wound—"

"In your throat?" he asked, unable to suppress his concern.

"My neck," I corrected, "and it only grazed me."

He gave me a frustrated look, and I spent the remainder of the drive to Washington, D.C. telling him what had happened to me and what it was like to work in one of Hitler's most cherished propaganda press agencies. When I finished, Bennett placed his hands on his temples and murmured, "I almost wish I hadn't heard all of that, dear. You could have been killed."

The chauffeur pulled up to our brick row home and saluted Bennett before letting us out, a grin on his face.

"Welcome back, Mrs. Sterling. I am glad you are safe."

"Thank you, Gerald," I replied, "and I hope you can come over for dinner soon. And bring your wife, okay?"

He smiled. "Yes, madam. Have a good evening!"

Bennett helped me hobble up the stairs and into the house, as if I were taking my first steps. It was charming.

The air inside smelled clean and fresh, unlike the stale, bomb-ridden air of my Munich flat. There were random pictures of me posted to various spots on the wall, with no apparent pattern to their placement. I folded one of the blankets scattered carelessly on the living room floor and cast Ben a sideways look.

"Did you sleep on the couch last night?"

"Just about half the night," he said sheepishly, "I was too excited and terrified of what news I might get today. And I was worried that someone might knock on the door with word of your arrival, and I didn't want to miss it."

I chuckled and jokingly knocked his officer's cap off his head.

"Now," he continued, holding my hand, "you need to lie down."

Shaking my head and smirking wickedly, I backed into the kitchen and opened our new mint green refrigerator, which I used to despise since it clashed with my favorite red curtains. It now felt like the perfect color.

"You can't possibly be hungry, Louella, after all you've been through!"

I gazed at him, as if the concept presented a challenge. "Well, I am," I shrugged, "and I—"

I gasped and pulled a pomegranate from the refrigerator, exclaiming, "You bought them!"

In one of the two letters I was able to send straight to Bennett without encrypting or keeping it purely professional, I mentioned my constant craving for pomegranates. The scarcity of fresh food in Germany had been excruciating, and my favorite fruit was absolutely unavailable in Munich, even on the black market.

He grinned, chuckled at my joy, and said, "Of course, dear! I would not deny my Cipher her desires." He kissed my palm and split open the bittersweet and bleeding fruit, dividing the seeds between us.

Ben offered me an unintentional crimson smile, juice flowing from his teeth and down his lips like he was a child.

I giggled and pulled him into a kiss across the table.

"I've never been so glad to see you happy," he said softly, tucking a strand of hair behind my ear.

"And I've never been happier."

He grabbed my hand and led me into the living room, where he put a record on the phonograph and let it play softly.

"May I have this dance, my darling?" he asked, a smirk on his lips as he gently pulled me to him. He sang the words, and I murmured softly along, taking in the scent of his clothes and allowing him to lead the dance.

The mere thought of you, the longing I feel for you

When I'm near you, time seems to slow down. I can see your face in every bloom.

Your eyes are in stars above

I'm simply thinking about you.

Just thinking about you, my love.

"I wish we could stay here forever," I said softly, tucking my head into his chest as we rocked back and forth.

He laughed, and I could hear his heartbeat.

"Maybe we should both leave our jobs, hmm? Create a victory garden and collect tin cans. Instead of being involved in plane crashes and going undercover in Germany, do normal war effort tasks."

"I don't know if I'll ever be able to return to normal life after this. Besides, I hate gardening."

I awakened next to Bennett in the middle of the night, his arms snugly wrapped around me. He would have to leave for a debriefing at the OSS at five a.m., and I would most likely not see him until tomorrow evening. The moonlight through our curtains illuminated our clock, which read 2:47. I slipped out from under his arms and stood up, my nightgown falling loosely as I shivered slightly. Bennett mumbled and turned over, but he didn't wake up. I wasn't accustomed to sleeping through the night; in Munich, we had air raids almost every night, and we were crammed into the basement with the other apartment dwellers while bombs shook above us.

Groggy, I walked into the bathroom, where Bennett's military uniform was displayed, and washed my face. My skin was very pale, and I had lost a lot of weight in Germany due to their ration system. Clothes that had previously fit well were now hanging loosely on my shoulders, and all of the muscle I'd worked so hard to build with Bennett had vanished.

I uncapped my dark crimson lipstick on the counter and delicately scrawled "I love you" on the mirror. Bennett hated the fact that he had to work the day after I returned, especially given the dreadful state he believed I was in. I was determined not to make him feel too awful about it. I removed my new bandage from my neck and studied the stitches, wincing as I brushed away a little blood. The knife wound in my side had healed wonderfully owing to Veronica Hart's medical assistance, but my fractured rib still hurt with every movement.

I took a deep breath and crawled back into bed, under Bennett's arm. He mumbled a bit and said, "Agent..."

I chuckled softly and kissed him on the cheek. "Get some sleep, Major General." He muttered something incoherent and pulled me close to his chest. I fell asleep in his arms, unsure if he was sleeping or half-awake.

The next morning, I woke to the faint morning light streaming through the drapes. A plate with eggs, a glass of milk, and a dish of leftover pomegranate seeds sat at the edge of the bed.

I grinned as I picked up the letter placed beneath the dish, written in Bennett's script.

"Hello, Darling.

I'm so sorry I couldn't stay with you; you know how uncomfortable I'll be at the office today without you. Hopefully, you'll be awake before this breakfast goes cold, but I've left some extra food downstairs for you if that's not the case. Don't forget about dinner with the President at 6 p.m.; dress formally. I will see you tonight, my darling. Don't leave the house without being ready to face the reporters; they're waiting at the end of our block. I'm so happy you're back.

Forever yours,

Bennett."

Under the dish of eggs, the newspaper was neatly folded into a square. There was a giant photo of Ben and me kissing at the airport with the caption, "The Cipher is Back!"

The caption behind the photo read, "Sterling's girl arrives from the warfront; emotional reunion strikes hearts all across America." I smiled and tucked it into the pocket of my bathrobe as I prepared for the day. I'd married a good man.

9

Chapter Nine

One month later.

A chilly touch on my shoulder caused me to jump from my workstation at the OSS, and Bennett's whispering voice behind me called out, "Agent." Grinning, I turned around and grabbed his collar, bringing our noses together. "Major General."

Ciaran Saunders, one of Ben's best friends and my office neighbor, laughed as he hurled a ballpoint pen at us.

"Would you save it for after work? How am I supposed to finish this report while you two are all doll-dizzy on me?"

Ben chuckled and nodded. "Agreed. You keep working; we'll go down to my office and continue there."

"Talk a little quieter," I muttered, locking my arm with his and looking around to see if anyone else had overheard. "You, of all people, should know that a scandal is the last thing we need."

He raised his eyebrows, and Ciaran glanced between us with interest.

"We're married, for heaven's sake, Lou!"

The three of us chuckled, and Ben added, "But in all seriousness, darling, they've called both of us for a meeting upstairs." I tilted my head and grabbed my bag, unrolling the paper from my typewriter and tucking it inside my desk to protect the classified information.

"Why? I've already debriefed them on my entire stay in Europe."

"Who knows," he said grimly, guiding me toward the stairs. I knew what he was thinking: *Please don't send her on another mission.* His desire to keep me close was touching, but we both knew it wouldn't last forever.

We entered the main meeting room to find a table full of generals, commanders, and cabinet members, some of whom I had never seen before. They stood respectfully as we entered, but the atmosphere was tense. Ben and I exchanged wordless glances.

"Is something wrong?" I asked quietly as we sat across from them.

"Good afternoon, Major General and Mrs. Sterling."

"Agent," Ben corrected softly.

"I'm sorry?"

He repeated louder, "Her name is *Agent* Sterling, sir."

There was an uncomfortable silence, but I was proud of Bennett for speaking up. I was often referred to as Mrs. Sterling since my superiors weren't comfortable with a woman carrying such a title. Usually, I didn't mind, but I knew it irritated Bennett to no end.

"Alright," one general said, "Agent. We wanted to ask you more about the concentration camp train you took in Munich. It states here that you jumped out of a train car full of Jews in a meadow near Stuttgart, is that correct?" I nodded slowly.

Another man added, "And this was early morning on October 2nd?" I nodded again, trying to figure out their angle. Ben shifted uncomfortably in his seat.

"Before your escape, was there any kind of lock on the outside?"

"Yes, it was a hefty padlock. I used Mr. Lane's new silenced handgun to get it off." I looked at Sidney Lane, one of my close friends and the scientist responsible for outfitting me with gadgets and chemicals on missions, but he stared uneasily at his hands.

"Mrs. Sterling," a man in a tweed suit said, "we've received reliable intelligence that every prisoner on that train was killed upon arrival at Natzweiler as punishment. They discovered a missing padlock and an open rail car."

I froze. Their words didn't feel real, and I tried to grasp what they were saying. *They all died.*

Bennett took a long breath and squeezed my hand under the table. "Are you blaming her for this? That's unjust, and you know it."

My breath caught in my throat, and I realized Bennett was wrong. It really *was* my fault.

"Do you have any doubt that this was your train, Mrs. Sterling?" I tried to respond, but fear rendered me silent. The man who spoke English, the girl I gave the soup to, the children, the mother fighting to get her baby a spot by the window, the father who lost all three of his daughters, the woman my age who dreamed of being a concert pianist, and the boy who just wanted to sit next to me. *Murdered.*

"How could she have known?" Bennett shouted, leaning forward angrily while I sat frozen. "She had just been viciously attacked by the Gestapo and risked her life to bring you information! How could we have known this would happen? For all we know, those prisoners were doomed regardless."

But I couldn't stop picturing them, panicking in the gas chambers.

"Did you not consider what the Germans would find when they arrived at Natzweiler, Mrs. Sterling? You took advantage of those prisoners' vulnerability to save yourself some time."

Bennett gripped my hand tightly, fuming, while I looked up at him. I didn't want to say anything for fear of breaking down, and I knew he understood. These men wouldn't listen to anything I said, but hearing it from my husband might make a difference.

"That's so far from the truth," Ben said passionately, "and you know it."

"Is it, Major General? Your wife's actions resulted in 700 men, women, and children being sent to the gas chambers. Do you understand—"

Ben shot to his feet, slamming his fist on the table. I flinched instinctively as if I'd heard a gunshot.

"That is enough." Ben said firmly. "Let's go, Louella." He gently pulled me to my feet. Numb and unable to hold back tears, I paused and looked back at the men before following Ben out the door.

"If I am to be removed," I said shakily, "I will accept it. But I never intended to hurt any of them. I'd give my life to bring just a few of them back."

I closed the door behind me and collapsed into Bennett's arms in the marble hallway, quietly sobbing. He held me close, running his hands through my hair, trying to comfort me.

"I killed them all," I whispered.

He cupped my face in his hands and looked me in the eye.

"Lou, listen to me. *You didn't do this.* Do you hear me? You are not responsible for those people's deaths."

But I couldn't stop crying. We both knew I was to blame, at least partially.

"Listen, darling," he said softly, "most of those men have never left the country. They don't know what it's like. They can't imagine what you've gone through."

He led me down another corridor and sat with me on a plush sofa.

"It's still my fault," I cried, leaning against him, letting him cradle me. "I'm not even worried about losing this job anymore. How can I ever face them again, knowing I'm responsible for hundreds of innocent deaths due to my own negligence?"

Bennett sighed. "You need to stop saying that. They were headed to Natzweiler, Louella. They weren't going to make it out of there." He shook his head. "What I'm trying to say is that they were doomed the moment they boarded that train. You admitted they could turn you in if their lives depended on it. We'll never know the truth, but you did everything you could, love."

He kissed my hand gently, smiling at me.

"It looks like we both have the evening off, though. How about dinner?"

I rested my head on his shoulder and groaned, "I'm not hungry."

"C'mon," he whispered, wiping a tear from my cheek. "Pretend to be in love with me. I'm just a desperate old schoolboy, remember?"

His facial expressions and terrible voice impressions were endearing, and I couldn't help but smile.

"Oh, bloody Nora," I sighed. "I'll go to dinner with you, but don't expect me to be thrilled about it. I just want to crawl into bed for the rest of my life and never speak to anyone again. Is that too much to ask?"

He grinned slightly and pulled me to my feet as we slowly made our way to the elevators.

"I'll see what I can do, Cipher." Bennett warmly wrapped his arm around me, tugging playfully on my brown locks.

That night, I tried my best to enjoy our dinner on the patio of Le Catalan in downtown Washington, DC.

Ben knew how much I was hurting from the news earlier, so he did everything he could to lighten the mood, especially by cracking absurd medical jokes and reminding me of all the wonderful memories we shared. Ben had been studying to be a doctor at Yale when the war broke out, and his strong belief in the Allied cause drove him to drop out and join the British army, just as I was leaving my unsatisfying job at a Philadelphia newspaper to join the British Air Force. We both knew how much he longed to return to medicine, but his promotion to such a high rank in the OSS had almost guaranteed him a life of politics and espionage until he retired. He made up for his lost career by trying to diagnose every ailment I ever had and telling the most terrible jokes about topics only he understood.

"Excuse me, Mister and Madame Sterling?" Someone behind me asked. "May I take your photograph for my newspaper?" A man in suspenders and a white shirt stood at the table behind us, holding a large camera. I looked at Bennett with amusement, and he gave the photographer a short nod.

"Thank you so much," the man said. "Now just keep eating, and pretend like I'm not here."

The reporter leaned over the aisle to get a good shot, his face full of admiration.

"Madame Sterling?" Bennett chuckled quietly as the man snapped our picture. "That's even better than Agent."

"Shh," I whispered, smiling. "Let's not offend the poor man; I think it's sweet."

The photographer approached, shook both of our hands, and asked, "Madame, may I ask who you're wearing tonight?"

Bennett raised an eyebrow at me, wondering if I wanted to continue, but I smiled and said, "This dress is an old Claire McCardell, one I've had for years. I haven't had much opportunity to shop lately, so I've happily returned to my old clothes. I enjoy giving them a modern twist." The man smiled as he jotted down my remarks.

"Would you say this is you doing your part in the war effort?" I hesitated.

My contribution to the war effort? I thought. I had gone underground in Munich, watched friends die in front of me, felt utterly alone for months, been stabbed, shot at, and beaten. I had lied about my age on my recruitment form and been shot down over France, narrowly surviving. My war effort had been a series of horrifying experiences, and part of me wondered if it would've been easier to die in that plane crash than live with the trauma. The war effort wasn't about reusing last season's evening gown—it was a nightmare.

I took a deep breath and replied, "Yes. We all must make sacrifices for our country. Textiles are needed on the battlefield, and we should be creative."

"Thank you," the man said, eyes gleaming. "I'll never forget this. Look for it in the Washington Chronicle tomorrow!" He thanked us profusely as he left, and Bennett stared at me incredulously. I raised a hand.

"I know what you're thinking. I'm thinking the same thing, but it could've been worse. Let's just eat our dessert."

Ben smirked and leaned closer. "Does he know who you are? How inconsiderate—"

"The poor man wasn't inconsiderate; he just wasn't thinking."

"Is there any difference?"

"The public doesn't know anything about what I've done. They never will."

He sipped his water and sighed.

"And they know every 'heroic' thing I've done, even though all I do is sit in an office. My job is waiting for the word that my wife has been shot in Paris or captured in Vienna. Or stabbed in Munich," he added, giving me a teasing smile.

"Just accept the praise, darling," I said. "And I'll accept being your fashionable housewife with rumors of spying in her past."

We gazed at each other with eyes that had seen too much. We both knew that even if the war ended tomorrow, our lives would never be the same again. The scars from battle and the emotional toll of our fame would never fully heal. People would always see me as the delicate wife of a Major General, but I didn't mind as much as he did. Bennett took a deep breath and said, "You could be the queen if you wanted to."

"I'd rather be yours."

10

Chapter Ten

"Lou?"

I brushed away my tears and turned to face Bennett, the moonlight revealing the worry on his drowsy face.

"I'm sorry to wake you," I said quietly, "but I'm fine."

He caressed one of my tightly curled pin curls and tilted his head.

"You didn't sound great. You were crying so hard you shook the bed."

"I'm sorry, but I'm okay, sweetie. It's just... every time I close my eyes, I see those Jews in the train car," I choked out as the tears flowed once again. "I can't handle the guilt anymore, Ben."

Despite his strong arms and stubborn expression, I could feel his shoulders weaken. He was well aware of how terrible the news had been for me, as shown by the events of the last few weeks. Every time I slept, I woke up screaming from a nightmare. Every time someone asked for my photo or recognized me from the papers, I felt like a hypocrite. I wasn't a hero; I was a killer. No better than the Nazis in Munich.

The OSS officers didn't dismiss me, but I almost wished they had. Every day, I lived in fear that someone would discover what had happened to those Jews and accuse me.

"You know what I'm going to say," Bennett muttered, rubbing my neck as he let me cry.

"It's not my fault," I sobbed. "I know. But—"

"What could you have done, Louella?" he asked. "Realistically, what could you have done to save those people you met on the train?"

I shook my head.

"I don't know. Ben, I could have just avoided taking the train in the first place. I was so scared of waiting any longer to get medical help for my side that I made a poor decision."

Bennett cupped my face in his hands and said, "You would have died if you'd waited any longer to get to Veronica Hart—"

"But that's the point," I said, hiccupping through my grief. "I lived, but seven hundred men, women, and children died because of me. And I escaped just in time for them all to suffer the consequences."

"They were already on their way to a camp. It's not like you could have just snuck them all out of Germany, Lou."

I fell silent. He was right, I thought, but then another idea hit me.

"What if we could've smuggled them out of Germany?"

"What?"

"You know that report we got a few weeks ago about the French Resistance member smuggling Jews from his home?"

Ben scoffed. "Yes, the one who was decapitated in front of his family. I see where this is going."

I sat up, switched on the little light by the bed, and looked at him intently. "Ben, the OSS is looking for an agent to infiltrate Marseille. Just think about it—helping to hide and transport Jews to safety in America or England, while feeding intelligence back to Washington D.C."

"You will not leave me again, Lou. Not to do something as foolish as that."

I giggled slightly and kissed him on the forehead. "That's why *you'll* come with me. Besides, I'm not as fluent in French as you are."

His eyes widened. "I can't—"

"We have to, darling. No one in America, except for people with classified knowledge, truly understands what's happening over there. If we don't act, we're no better than the Krauts beheading people and sending innocent children to these camps."

"Do you have any idea how dangerous Marseille is, Louella? It's one of the most perilous cities in the world."

I laughed. "And Munich is the most dangerous city in the world, and I survived. We can handle anything. Imagine if we bought a little house where you opened a small medical practice downstairs. Jews could come in using a secret code, and we could offer them food, a clean bed, and good company before sending them off with ration cards and forged IDs. We could save lives."

"I get that you want to make up for what happened to the people on that train, Lou," Ben groaned, rubbing his temples. "But this... this is impossible. I'm the Head of Intelligence here, Louella. I can't just run off with my wife on a field mission in France, even if I thought it was a good idea."

A dog growled outside, and I jumped, reminded of the vicious attack dogs that patrolled the streets with German soldiers in Munich. Bennett glanced at me, as if to say, *That's my point.*

"I can't stay here, Ben. You haven't seen what I've seen. Something has to be done, and we're the only ones who can do it. Let me talk to the OSS tomorrow, okay? Just get some rest."

He groaned.

"So, I'll have no choice but to agree in the morning?"

"Exactly."

The next day, I stormed into Allan Goldstein's office with a cup of hot coffee. He raised an eyebrow as I set it down and said, "Good day, Mr. Goldstein. And how's Europe today?"

"On fire, as usual. What's going on, Agent?"

Goldstein was the head of the OSS's Secret Intelligence Branch, responsible for coordinating with American and European resistance forces and forming a vast anti-Nazi intelligence network. I had worked with him extensively before my mission in Munich, and he was the one who passed most of my messages to Bennett. Now, he was the one I needed.

"I need your help." He smirked and took a sip of coffee.

"What a surprise. Where are you planning to go this month, Louella? Africa? Japan? Hitler's bunker?"

"Marseille, France."

I sat in the chair across from his desk and looked at him pleadingly. Despite his sarcasm, I knew he'd be receptive to my request. If I could get his approval, the mission would happen, and Bennett would have to join me.

"You want to go to occupied France. Wasn't Munich enough?"

I exhaled. "You need someone on the inside. The French government has been pleading for the liberation of Marseille. You know how important that port is to our cause, and the only way we can take it back is if you have someone on the ground."

I watched his reaction as I outlined my plan. He seemed impressed by how well I'd thought it through, like my best talent was brewing coffee.

"What does Sterling say?"

"He'll come around—if you agree to back this plan."

Allan Goldstein rested his hand on his brow and leaned forward.

"You know it's against OSS policy to let married couples work in the same theater of war. We've already bent the rules for you two."

"So, you follow *all* the rules here? Could've fooled me."

He sighed. "It'll take a lot more than my endorsement to make this happen."

"I know. Just talk to Mr. Shepardson and see if you can get it approved. If I have to spend the rest of my life fetching coffee or listening to Ciaran talk about his latest hunting trip, I think I'll lose my mind. Please."

"I'll speak to him. Now, get back to work, Agent. Why don't you do some research on the area and figure out where we could post you in Marseille?"

Grinning, I pulled out three written pages of intel I'd gathered that morning, detailing local businesses, thriving industries, Resistance members in the region, homes for sale, and countless other bits of information they'd need to know.

Goldstein blinked and quietly flipped through the pages. "How long did this take you?"

"Just this morning. I was the only one in the library, so I got a lot done."

"I can see that," he said, looking up at me with a small smile. "And I'll push this through. Besides your famous face, Louella, you're the best operative for the job. Shepardson will agree."

I thanked him and left his office with high hopes. The fact that Bennett would be going with me would only strengthen my case, and hopefully, he'd warm up to the idea once everyone else was on board.

Back at my desk down the hall, I looked up at Ciaran Saunders, who was staring at me expectantly.

"What'd he say?"

"He's going to talk to Mr. Shepardson and try to convince Ben. You can call me Madame Sterling from now on." He laughed and gave me a sideways look.

"I'm happy for you," he said with his slight Southern drawl, "but if they put someone else at your desk while you're gone, I'll quit. No one else would let me take my shoes off while I'm working except you."

I rolled my eyes.

"I'm going to pick up my mail from downstairs," I said, carefully getting to my feet. "Want me to grab yours?"

"Come on, Louella. You're too sweet for this job. Would you?"

"You bet."

On my way back from the mailroom with a large package for Ciaran and a few letters for Bennett, I heard someone say, "Hey, dolly! I've got a job for you."

Indignant, I glanced back to see two men in their late forties grinning at me.

"What did you call me?"

"I called you Dolly," one of them said, pointing to a stack of papers on his desk. "And I need you to fill these forms out for me."

"You can call me Agent. And that's not my job."

They rolled their eyes, and I felt my cheeks heat up as the entire Research and Analysis section turned to listen, the clacking of typewriters barely masking their eavesdropping.

"Listen, honey, we're real agents with work to do. If you don't do your job, we'll report you. Secretaries aren't agents, sweetheart. But you sure are cute."

He slapped me hard on the rear, and I froze. Someone gasped. Fuming, I walked up to their desks and bent down to look them in the eyes.

"My name is Louella Sterling," I said quietly. "I'm a special agent in the Secret Intelligence branch down the hall. Not only am I your superior here, but I also outrank you on the battlefield—not that you've ever been there. That trick may have worked with the ladies here who would lose their jobs if they spoke up, but not with me. Be thankful we're in a public place right now, boys, because otherwise, you'd be unconscious."

They exchanged looks.

Standing up with a honeyed smile, I asked, "What's your name?"

The first man avoided my gaze and didn't respond, so I picked up a paper from his desk.

"John Marlow, is it? And you?" I turned to the other man.

He smirked and shook his head. "You're crazy if you think I'm tellin' you my name—"

An exhausted-looking woman my age appeared behind him, holding three empty coffee cups. She muttered, "McCall. His name is Bruce McCall, Agent Sterling."

I grinned as the man looked stunned by the turn of events.

"Thank you," I said sincerely to her, a shared understanding passing between us that these men would never comprehend. "Mr. McCall, Mr. Marlow," I continued, taking a deep breath, "it's been a pleasure."

11

Chapter Eleven

I sat on the seat along the side of the women's 'workout gym,' breathing hard, and checked my cracked knuckles. The punching bag I was using swung strongly from the ceiling, as if ready for another strike. I rose back up, kicking my brown military-issue Oxford heels out of the way after wiping away the blood on my hands, perspiration on my forehead, and tears in my eyes. The men's training facility in the basement was far better than the women's, so I sometimes took one of their punching bags to practice on my own. Today, I went to the gym because I was angry.

I repeatedly struck the bag hard. Tears of anger flowed down my cheeks, and I realized I should have bandaged my knuckles first. However, the pain felt better with bloodied hands. Those men would always outperform me, no matter how much I accomplished, where I traveled, or how many lives I saved. I would never be appreciated or treated well in any workplace. The shame and frustration I had been suppressing for months suddenly felt real, and I wished things weren't always so difficult.

"Louella."

My heart sank. Without looking around, I recognized Bennett.

"This is the women's gym, Ben," I said solemnly, punching the bag without looking at him. He ignored my words and grabbed me by the shoulders.

"Is it true?" I sighed and drew away, and he understood what it was. That was all he needed to know.

"I'm gonna kill them," he said, heading back toward the door with his hands at his side.

I grabbed him quickly and turned him around to face me.

"No, you are not. Just calm down."

"Are you crazy?" he shouted, raising his voice so loudly that I took a step back. "They have humiliated and hurt you. If they think they can get away with—"

I grabbed his uniform and tried to catch his attention.

"I handled it, okay?"

"By doing nothing."

"I can't fix everything with my fists like you can, Ben. It's handled."

"How?"

I crossed my arms in front of him and smiled slightly, saying, "They forgot I was their employer. And I outrank them."

"Did you get someone to fire them?"

I shook my head. "They'll come in tomorrow morning with a stack of paperwork on their desks about this high," I said, gesturing with my hands. "If they're so interested in women in the workplace, they'll have to see how women actually work."

Bennett raised his eyebrows and smiled wickedly. "You gave them all the filing that people always give you, didn't you?"

I nodded. "And not just mine. When I asked some of the other women if they wanted any work done, there was a large turnout. Surprisingly, much of it had not been given to them in the first place," I added sarcastically, walking over to the seat and putting on my green military jacket over my brown skirt and white button-up.

"And not a single punch was thrown," I said, staring at him as he started wrapping my damaged hands in white strips of fabric from my bag. He groaned, finished the wrapping, and kissed my hands.

"I get your point. You amaze me."

Bennett held the door open for me as I slid back into my heels, and I placed my arm in his as we walked outside to the building housing Bennett and the other senior officials' offices.

"Are people talking?"

"Not much. They're all afraid of you, I guess. And Ciaran has spent the whole day tormenting anybody who asks where you went. Also, what did Allan Goldstein say about the two of us traveling to Marseilles?"

I shrugged. "He seemed to support it," I grinned as Bennett rolled his eyes slightly, "and he's going to discuss it with Mr. Shepardson. Has your opinion changed?"

"A bit, I suppose," he said, "but I still think it's a terrible idea. The only difference today is that I believe it's a bad idea that we should at least explore."

I giggled and paused outside his large office, allowing him to gently grasp my hands.

"I wish I didn't have this job, Louella. You work twice as hard as me, but you have to share a desk with Ciaran 'take my shoes off during work'

Saunders while doing everyone else's job. Nobody except the Joint Chiefs of Staff and I will ever know how much you've contributed to this war, and I'm expected to be OK with sitting in this large office all day while you're tormented by Technical Sergeants in the Research department outside? You deserve better than this."

I placed a finger on his lips and forced a smile.

"It doesn't matter whether I deserve anything, Ben. I get to work with my handsome guy in my dream job... aside from flying planes, of course. I have it so much better than others in this building, let alone around the world."

"But that doesn't make the lack of respect you're given acceptable, Lou."

"Not everything has to be fair all the time," I replied with a tiny giggle, "despite what every man in this office seems to believe. Come on, we have two hours left in the workday. I'll meet you outside at 7 p.m., okay?"

He kissed my cheek, looked around at the others watching, and smiled mischievously.

"I'll be there at 6:50."

The next week, we got news that our transfer request had been accepted, and we were sent to Camp X, a British and American training center in Canada known for "assassination and elimination" agents. Bennett was more afraid than I was, even though he had undergone his original training there years before. Over the next three months, we studied sabotage methods, subversion, explosives training, radio communications, encoding and decoding (which we already knew a lot about), and the art of silent killing and unarmed combat. Our classmates were new recruits to the OSS, including many women, so we had already learned and applied many of the concepts we were being taught. Still, we benefited much from our individual instruction in French colloquialisms, Marseilles culture and traditions, parachuting over occupied territory, and our new identities, which we would soon assume.

Bennett was now Alain Girard, a respected doctor moving to Marseilles to establish a practice in the heart of the port city. He would tint his hair a rich brown and wear glasses, which, to our surprise, improved his eyesight slightly. Born on August 24, 1919, in Cannes, a city just west of Marseilles, his father was killed in the Great War just before his birth, and his mother died from a broken heart when he was two years old.

My name was Louise Girard, Alain's youthful and beautiful wife. After much deliberation, it was decided that Louise was raised at a boarding school in Germany, which would explain my ability in the language if I ever needed to use it. My natural blonde hair would resurface, but they insisted on tinting it red and cutting it just below my shoulders. We determined it was too dangerous for me to get contacts to conceal my well-known green eyes, but I would try to wear sunglasses as much as possible when running errands and wear heels as much as possible to increase my height.

"Louella," Bennett said as we finished our last daily run around Lake Ontario before leaving the camp, "what will you do if someone asks about the scar on your neck from that gunshot in Herrsching?"

I grinned, pulling at my military-issue jeans, which were three sizes too small.

"I fell out of a treehouse when I was a child and cut myself."

"Sounds believable enough, I guess," he panted, stopping behind a tree and checking his watch, "but what if they ask about the wound on your stomach?"

I gasped and playfully punched him, laughing with him at the absurdity of anyone ever seeing that scar.

"If that happens, they'll be dead before they can even ask."

Bennett laughed as we returned to the camp dorms, soaking in every sight and scent we could. He wrapped his arm around me, and I sighed.

"I'm so scared."

"Me too."

We planned to head back to Washington that afternoon to get a few things in order before leaving for France the next morning when we would be dropped from a plane into occupied territory.

"Hey," someone shouted from across the courtyard as we were about to enter the main training facility, "were you gonna leave without saying goodbye?"

Wing Commander Drew, a British SOE operative, writer, and fighter pilot, slept in the room across from Bennett. We'd been close friends with him since we arrived at Camp X, and he seemed to have an unmatched ability to tell stories.

"Reginald," Bennett called to him, hurrying up and sincerely shaking his hand, "I'm glad to see you. Yeah, we're getting our bags as we speak. You could come with us if you want."

He grinned, bowed, and kissed my hand, adding, "Agent Sterling, looking as dashing as ever. Don't let those folks in France get a glimpse of you."

Bennett and I exchanged amused looks at his English candor, and I responded, laughing, "I'll do my best, Wing Commander Drew. Have you heard anything more from your publisher regarding *The Gremlins*?"

He shook his head and followed us up the stairs to where our packed bags were.

"The RAF pilots and your First Lady seem to like the book," he said with pride, "but it's hard to get any news inside this rot some cave-hole."

We chuckled, and he accompanied us to the small airport just outside the property, where he told us about his future book ideas.

"Now I have a question for a story I'm thinking of that needs a truly honest answer," he added, turning to face us and walking backward toward the plane. "Which do you think you'd like better: snozzberries or fizzlecrumps?"

I wrinkled my brow, and Bennett and I shared another smile.

"What even are those things?"

Reginald rolled his eyes, as if it were so obvious.

"They're not actual things yet," he added, "but they'll be in my universe one day. C'mon," he said as we approached the plane, "which one sounds the most scrumdiddlyumptious?"

I chuckled, and Bennett said above the boom of the engine, "Definitely snozzberries. Do you agree, Louella?"

"Sure," I said, holding my hair back as the wind whipped through the air, "because it sounds nicer. Fizzlecrumps seem like dull, stale cookies that toddlers wouldn't like as much as fruit, right?"

Drew grinned. "Then it is decided. Good luck, both of you."

"Thank you, sir," Bennett responded. "We will do our best. Thank you for all your help, and best wishes to you as well."

We boarded the plane, and Ben held my hand as we took our seats on the side.

"Are you ready?"

"No. But I am excited."

12

Chapter Twelve

Sleet started to fall outside as I peered tensely out our bedroom window, the Washington DC roadway below us gradually dying down as night fell. We had already packed everything we could parachute down with and met with authorities for our last briefing. All that remained was to see Sidney Lane, our "gadget man," tomorrow to get our new firearms and anything else he had created for us. Then we would leave the protection of the United States for possibly years.

"You know," Bennett began from the bathroom, shaving cream all over his face, "we don't have to sit here and sulk the whole night. This is our last night in America for who knows how long! We could bake something," he said weakly. I turned around to sneer at him.

"Bake something? What kind of adventure is that? But I like the idea," I thought, jumping over the bed and digging through my clothes, "of doing something fun."

He emerged from the restroom with furrowed eyebrows and a half-shaven face.

"Let's go dancing."

"No way," Ben laughed, "I'm not going to have us recognized by the press the night before going to France. The last thing you need is a photograph of your latest appearance in the paper." I rolled my eyes and raced to his side, pulling on his pajama top.

"I'll wear a wig and a different color lipstick. It's not like we aren't experienced with a good old-fashioned cover. And this one would be easy compared to every other cover we've ever made. I promise it'll be fun, sweetheart."

"I'm sure it would be fun," he laughed, "but I don't think it would be wise."

"We don't need to speak to anybody; we can just dance and eat. We haven't gone out in a long time, and I believe Buddy Garland is performing tonight at the Madison Club. Please."

He cleaned his face, kissed me on the forehead, looked up at the sky, and shrugged; I knew he'd have to agree.

"They told us not to leave the house."

I rolled my eyes: "They also advised you not to shave, and I can see you're obeying that guideline very beautifully, hmm? C'mon, you can wear a great suit while I wear my red dress. If we stay here any longer, we'll die of dread, regret, and fear."

"Fine. But if they play *Sing, Sing, Sing*," Bennett sighed, pointing to me with a smile as he unbuttoned his pajama shirt and put on a white button-down, "you must let me toss you up at least once."

I laughed and sobbed, saying, "I kicked you in the face last time!"

"Yes," he said with a faint smile, "but we defeated that arrogant lawyer and his girlfriend. The audience loved it."

"This isn't a jitterbug contest, Ben," I told him as I slid into my dress, "just a night out like normal people have."

"Either way, we're gonna win."

I rolled my eyes.

Thirty minutes later, we were strolling arm in arm down the dimly lit street to the Madison Club, which was just a few streets from our old row home. I was wearing one of the several wigs I'd gathered while doing domestic intelligence operations, and I changed from my preferred deep red lipstick to a brighter, pinker tint that would be less recognized. Bennett was dressed in a fine brown suit jacket he had acquired from a charity shop in Dublin, Ireland, and the same olive-green sweater he wore when we first met in France. Fortunately, someone was able to remove the bloodstains.

The thick-rimmed spectacles he always refused to wear, along with the slicked-back golden hair peeking out from his hat, provided him just enough of a disguise to mix in with the rest of the men in the club.

"Oh no," he murmured as we reached the massive edifice, yanking me back by the elbow. "They've got someone at the door checking tickets."

I chuckled and thought, *That won't be a problem, dear. Simply tell the guy who we are, and he will let us in.*

Bennett's eyes widened; he was always careful, and we complemented each other well.

"We won't tell anybody who we are, Louella! That was the whole reason I said we could go! You're wearing a wig, for goodness' sake!"

"Oh, stop," I responded, waving my hand. "He's much too busy to tell everyone anyhow. They won't care."

He grasped my arm and grinned slightly, placing his fingers on my face.

"You're insane. I've got a better idea."

I sprang into a limping run and followed him into the alley, laughing.

"I'm in heels, Bennett," I whispered loudly, "and my legs are killing me!"

Even after three years, the damage to my legs from the aircraft accident resurfaced on occasion, causing excruciating pain. Bennett reached back and grabbed my hand as he lifted himself up the rickety fire escape.

"Excuses, excuses," he crooned, imitating one of the trainers we'd met at Camp X. I stepped over the metal railing and followed him up the stairs to the fifth level. Sure enough, the window was open, and the curtains were flapping in the brisk November breeze. I glanced at him in surprise.

"How did you—"

"I used to carry newspapers to this building in 1933, and it was the last stop on my route. For years, my friends and I would go up the fire escape to the 16th story, where an elderly woman resided." He grinned as he assisted me through the window. "She always left the window unlocked, and her kitchen was the first room we came to, so we ate like royalty."

I gasped and smacked him on the shoulder. "That's terrible!"

"Every time I pass this building, I look up to see which windows are open out of curiosity." I rolled my eyes and followed him into the dull waiting room we found ourselves in.

"So," I said, "now what? Do we simply locate some steps and pretend like we've been here all along?"

Ben shrugged and opened the door to the hallway, beginning to reply when we both realized it wasn't a hallway. Instead, we came face to face with Buddy Garland himself, dressed in a bathrobe and holding his clarinet reed in one hand and a comb in the other. My jaw dropped, and Bennett froze.

Of course, I thought, envisioning what a fantastic story this would make later.

"Oh, sir, I am so sorry," Bennett began, grabbing my hand and starting to walk backward toward the fire escape. "We just—"

"Are you Major-General Sterling?" We exchanged looks as the legendary musician stared between us, his eyes wild.

"Oh, no," Ben stuttered over his words. "I believe you are thinking of someone else. We just—"

I stepped in front of him and smiled. "Yes, sir, he is."

Bennett stared at me as if I had just signed away our lives.

"We didn't want to cause a disturbance or be recognized out front, so we decided the fire escape would be a suitable alternative. Please excuse us; we didn't realize you were in here. We'll leave."

Mr. Garland put out his hand and smiled. "It's fine. In fact, I'm glad to finally meet you two. I often read about your exploits in the newspapers and listen to radio broadcasts about you. I won't ask you any more questions for fear of disclosing anything private, but would you like to wash up in my dressing room? You both," he smiled, gesturing to our disheveled attire, "look like you just climbed through a fire escape at the Madison Club... and we don't need that for the Cipher and the Head of Intelligence."

Bennett and I exchanged puzzled looks.

"We don't want to intrude," I said, adjusting my clothing and hoping he couldn't tell I was wearing a wig. "I'm sure you have to be ready to play out there in a little while. But if we might ask one question, how did you know it was us?"

He smiled, and I could see Bennett wasn't sure how to take the conversation; he was so used to being in command and having complete control over a situation.

"Your chemistry with each other is undeniable. You two just look like a pair. And you were both caught off guard when you saw me, so don't blame yourselves too much. You don't resemble the famous Sterlings, I guarantee."

We thanked him warmly, and he showed us the stairs that would take us to an inconspicuous entrance to the main floor.

"I won't tell a soul that you're here," he smirked, "but I'd love to see you two on the dance floor, yeah?"

"We'll be there if you play *Sing, Sing, Sing*," I said. "I've already promised him a dance."

Once inside the packed, high-end club, Bennett and I split off to avoid being seen wandering around together, and we met on the side, where a tiny diner-style bar was set up.

"Can I get you anything to drink?" the bartender inquired of Bennett.

"Oh, no, thank you," he said with a slight Southern accent.

"How about your girl?" the bartender said, gesturing to me. "How about something for her?"

I faked a grin and replied for myself, "I'll have some water."

The bartender started to giggle and glanced between the two of us. "You're contributing to the war effort, huh? Comin' right up."

He moved away, and Bennett and I exchanged looks. Whether the war required supplies or not, neither of us drank, but we didn't want to stand out and be noticed by this guy, who might easily identify us if he looked long enough. When he left and the opening band played to a crescendo that allowed us to speak without being overheard, I asked, "Have you been practicing your German?"

"Not as much as you've been practicing French, I'm guessing. Can you possibly imagine that? Hiding in plain sight on Nazi territory?"

"I can do more than you imagine, darling," I said, laughing slightly. "I've lived it. Once you get through the first few weeks, it seems like you're really living the life we're pretending to have. And it's terrifying."

Bennett pulled on my locks in the low light and smiled, his sleepy eyes gleaming with affection.

"Lou, you are much braver than me. I have a desk job."

"One of the most important desk jobs in America," I said.

"But I still have a desk job, where I file papers and listen to people bicker all day. And you're going throughout Europe, risking your life, really helping to win the war. How am I going to endure France with you?"

I offered a little bow to the bartender as he pushed two cups of water toward us and grasped Bennett's hand. "You don't give yourself enough credit. Have you forgotten what you did in Ireland and France before we met? Or your job catching the spy in Baltimore? And what about the enormous number of people you're responsible for as America's Director of Intelligence? Marseille will be a breeze. Besides, aren't you excited to go back into medicine?"

"Of course I am," he murmured, "but not operating on Nazis who threw out their backs vandalizing a bar."

I chuckled and said, "You have a point."

Buddy Garland and his band started to set up on the stage near the dance floor, and he winked at us with a tiny smile. A man in a huge suit walked on stage and introduced them, eliciting loud cheers from the audience. "Here's the first one," he said, "it's Buddy Garland and his band playing *Sing, Sing, Sing*."

Buddy Garland, who was in the front row, chuckled slightly when he observed our reaction and urged over the microphone, "Come on now, everyone! I want everyone on the dance floor."

Ben grabbed my hand and led me to the front, where the crowd started to gather.

"May I?" He bowed, a wry grin on his lips, and threw one arm around my waist, holding my hand with the other, as we both began to spin in rhythm with the music. He spun me around, and we fell back into each other's arms, repeating the move at breakneck speed. Everyone else was doing something similar, tossing their partners or showing off their most sophisticated steps.

Bennett and I had danced hundreds of times around America and Europe, and we were certain we could amaze the crowd, but our goal tonight was to stay unnoticed. We were both giggling hysterically as the famous song picked up speed and we desperately tried to keep up with the rhythm, swinging our arms and feet wildly.

"Tandem?" I asked as he turned me around.

He nodded, and I locked my arm with his for a brief second before spinning back in front of him. Someone whooped, and we moved our feet and hands in sync, as if we were riding a tandem bicycle.

Buddy Garland noticed us and raised his eyebrows. The fast tempo of the music caused people on the sidelines to start clapping along. Bennett and I continued to Lindy Hop until the song's mood shifted, and drums took over. I took a moment to catch my breath and muttered, "Are we going aerial?"

"Let's do it."

Garland's clarinet took over the song, and when I was ready, I nodded to Bennett and let him lift me from the swing so that I could stand by him. He hoisted me up with one hand while keeping me balanced with the other, and I sailed over his shoulders before landing on his left side.

A small crowd had gathered around us, cheering loudly, and Ben and I exchanged looks of resigned joy.

"Let's just hope my wig doesn't fall off," I whispered in his ear as we danced, our faces inches apart. We spun away from each other, and another man grabbed my hand, taking Bennett's place. I saw another woman take Ben's hand, and we exchanged amused smiles. My new partner tried to lead the way and swing me like Bennett, but he wasn't as skilled.

"You're a ducky shin-cracker if I ever saw one," he panted, struggling to keep up with me.

I raised an eyebrow. "I've been to my fair share of swing clubs in my day."

"So, sugar, are you rationed?"

I giggled. "Married."

His eyes dropped, and he glanced shyly at Bennett, who was dancing with the woman.

"It's fine," I reassured him. "He won't mind. Do you know the woman he's dancing with?"

"She's a friend of my cousin's. I'm sure she won't mean anything by it."

"Don't worry about us. Have you ever done an aerial?"

He stared at me with wide eyes and shook his head. I knew I should have ended the conversation long ago to protect my identity, but I felt sorry for the unfortunate young man.

"I'll help you; you don't need to toss me high. Impress that girl over there... she's watching you," I said, gesturing to a brunette standing at the edge of the room.

I helped him get his hands in the right place and jumped as high as I could to assist him; he stumbled a bit, but I caught myself and landed lightly on the ground as the song ended. Bewildered, he ran his hands through his hair and tried to hide his surprise.

"Golly," he muttered, "you're good." The crowd applauded as the dancers dispersed and a softer tune began to play.

"What's your name?" he asked, smiling at Bennett as he approached with the woman he'd been dancing with.

I gave Bennett a quick glance to see if he'd already given me a false identity for the woman, and he promptly replied, "Louise Girard. My sweetheart."

"And this is Alain Girard," I added, nodding at him. "My sweetheart."

They thanked us and walked away, clearly disappointed by how things had turned out but grateful that we had been kind to them. Bennett took my hand and led me back to the dance floor, holding me close as we swayed to the music. I could feel his chest rise as he chuckled, "I feel bad for those poor kids. That was me at Yale, you know. I wanted the attention of every girl I could find. And then, just when I had given up hope, my sweetheart dropped from the skies."

I smacked his arm playfully and rested my head on his chest. "There will never be anyone for me but you."

13

Chapter Thirteen

"We're approaching the drop site now," the copilot said from the cockpit, "so get ready to open the door."

I stared through the frost-covered glass at the Pyrenees mountains below us, and Bennett grasped my hand.

"You alright?"

I nodded, more to convince myself than him.

"I'm fine. I fly aircraft, so this shouldn't be an issue. And there's snow at the bottom—much softer than anything I've ever landed on."

Ben lifted his eyebrows and kissed my cheek lightly, adding, "It's okay to be afraid, Lou."

We both understood it wasn't the act of jumping out of the aircraft that concerned me, but my prior experience falling from the skies above France. That parachute had failed due to carelessness by those in command; who was to say this one would be any different? I shook off the sickening sensation in my stomach and put on my pack with the little clothing and equipment we were authorized to carry into Marseilles. Bennett did the same.

"Jump whenever you're ready," the pilot said, "and good luck down there. Thank you for what you're doing."

He saluted Ben and me as we opened the heavy door, and I grabbed my husband's hand.

"For liberty?" I yanked on his leather jacket and donned my goggles.

"For liberty." Why we were doing any of this.

We leaped nearly simultaneously, the wind whipping around us. My heart was pounding as the frigid air sliced through my flying suit. The mountains that separated Spain and France seemed to fall toward us in my vision, and I couldn't stop thinking about the aircraft disaster.

The screams of the people on the radio, the feel of Muriel's blood trickling from my hands amid the wreckage, and Bennett's dazed expression overwhelmed my senses. I clutched his hand even closer. After what seemed like an eternity, we pulled our parachutes, and our fast fall became serene and oddly quiet. I struck the snow on my hands and knees, trembling with shock. Bennett landed a few feet away, turned onto his back, and gazed up at the pink sky as dawn broke over the mountains.

"We made it."

"Not yet," he panted, pulling me up and removing my parachute, "we still have to get out of the mountains alive."

"Oh, please," I responded, "that's simple."

I woke to Bennett's cold lips on my nose, and he said quietly, "Bonjour, mon chérie. And welcome to your first day as a French lady!"

"Gah!" I gasped, squirming away from his touch. "Why are you so cold? Get off me, icicle!" I turned over, pulling the cover up to my neck, and Bennett chuckled. It was one a.m. back in Washington. We had landed in Port Vendrés at the foot of the Pyrenees yesterday, and a Resistance member with a boat had given us a lift across the Mediterranean to Marseilles.

We were then directed to the flat above Bennett's new medical practice in the Old Marseilles neighborhood, where we silently moved in without causing a disturbance or raising suspicion. Everyone assumed that another doctor and his wife had arrived in town, hoping for better results.

Bennett pulled me out of bed and offered me one of the few outfits I had packed for Europe.

"I just came back from the market," he said, "to get some food for breakfast today and buy some bug poison."

My eyes narrowed. "What bugs?"

"I took care of it, I promise. You do not want me to tell you where they were this morning."

I shrieked in disgust and pulled my light pink dress over my head.

"What's the plan now?"

"I don't know. Meet your neighbors? Purchase a stethoscope? Inconspicuously investigate the port's weak points and fortifications?"

I smirked and pushed Bennett's fake identity cards into his hand while laughing. "Then let's get to it, Alain."

"Will you do me the honor, Louise, of allowing me to escort you downstairs?"

I smiled and took his arm as he led me into the empty basement that would soon become his doctor's office.

Just as we were about to leave, the doorbell rang.

"I didn't even know we had a bell," Bennett said in French, going to open the door. I grabbed his arm and gave him a look.

"Let's be a little more cautious, shall we?" I reached for the handgun hidden in my stockings and held it by my side, out of sight of whomever was on the other side of the door.

After nodding at Ben, he opened the door.

"Monsieur and Madame Girard?" a man possibly in his forties asked.

"Yes, that's us. How can we help you?"

"My name is Gerard Dupont; I will be your contact and case officer here in Marseilles."

We exchanged apprehensive looks, and I gripped the gun tighter. The OSS had never assigned us a case officer, and we had never heard of him before. Could our cover have been blown so quickly?

"I'm sorry," I answered, "but we don't understand what you're talking about. Good day, sir."

I started to close the door, but he pulled it open, accidentally banging my head against it. Bennett's eyes flashed with rage. This would not end well.

"Louella and Bennett Sterling," the man stated, causing us to stop, "the Cipher of the Allies and the US Director of Intelligence. I am a Resistance commander and have been in communication with your OSS colleagues for quite some time. I know who you are; don't you think you should hear what I have to say?"

Bennett and I exchanged looks.

"Come in," I said, offering him the gun and motioning for him to follow Ben upstairs.

When he was sitting on one of the old couches that came with the flat, he added, "I'm your liaison with the Resistance. I just came here to let you know that I am available to assist you with anything you need."

I cocked the gun and held it to his head, though we all knew I wasn't going to fire. His story sounded believable.

"If you know who we are, why didn't they tell us about you in training?"

"You think they tell you two everything?"

Ben stepped forward. "I'm the head of US intelligence—"

"Who is now working as a field operative under my jurisdiction," he interrupted, to Bennett's annoyance. "I would advise you to remember that we are no longer in the District of Columbia, Monsieur Sterling."

Bennett looked at me with angry eyes. He wasn't used to being insulted like I was.

"This guy," he said to me in English, "has no clue what he's talking about. If the OSS wanted us to have a contact, they would have let us know. And they certainly wouldn't have chosen this guy."

"I speak English." We both looked at him in silence, and I raised my eyebrows.

"Fine," Bennett groaned. "We can speak German. Let's speak in German."

I shot him a glance and rolled my eyes.

"Do we have any choice but to believe him? He knows everything about us."

"Well forgive me for not trusting every pompous Socialist that comes barging into our house," he gestured to Dupont, spit flying from his lips as he aggressively spat the words in German, "demanding that we give him all of our intelligence!"

"Quiet down, would you?" I remarked softly, placing my hand on his arm. "I agree with you, but what else are we going to do? We need him, and his story is credible. How are we going to convince Resistance members and Jews to trust us without him?" I paused. "And what about our daily needs? The OSS was irresponsible not to inform us, Ben, but at least we have an ally now."

He exhaled and crossed his arms.

"A lousy ally if I've ever seen one. But you're right, I suppose."

Turning back to Dupont, Bennett stated in French, "We have decided, reluctantly, to trust you. What now?"

Dupont raised an eyebrow and leaned back.

"First, you must stop contradicting me. I'm in charge here. Second, expect a Resistance member in their mid-twenties to visit your doctor's office in two weeks. They will complain about a sore ear and a broken thumb, and once identified as a member of the Resistance, they will stay with you for three days before departing for Spain. You have a secret room in this house, correct?"

Bennett and I exchanged skeptical looks.

"Is there a secret room?"

"Why would we—"

Dupont placed his hand on his forehead and sighed loudly, as if we were the dumbest people he'd ever met.

"You'll have to work on it before they arrive. They said you two had that covered."

"Who's 'they'?"

"The OSS. They suggested you could build fake walls, hidden beds, and other things like that."

Ben rolled his eyes. "We can do it. But, just in case you forgot, we arrived last night. Not everyone can make everything perfect in an instant like you, okay? Give us time; we'll be ready when they arrive."

Dupont stood up and said, "Right. It was...interesting to meet you two; I'll see myself out. We'll be in contact."

On his way to the stairs, he peeked his head out and tilted it at me.

"So, your husband is a doctor...what are you?" he asked me quietly. "Where will you work?"

The question surprised both of us.

"I, um, won't work," I said hesitantly, "because it would draw too much attention. What are you getting at?"

"Madame Sterling, we could use you in the Resistance. It wouldn't be a full-time commitment, but you'd be helpful to the cause."

"Absolutely not," Bennett replied, "and it's Madame Girard now."

"Sir, I have to agree. That is not my role here, and I do not want to work for the Socialists who are to blame for so many of the problems the Allies have fought so hard to solve." I stopped and narrowed my eyes at Dupont.

"What would I be doing?"

Ben stared at me as if I had just ordered him to shove me off a bridge.

"Sabotaging trains," added Dupont, "flying planes if necessary, organizing supplies and munitions, and possibly assisting in any...conflicts that may arise."

"So if your organization goes rogue again and kills more French politicians, she'll be the one with her head in a basket?" Bennett answered curtly, "No thanks. Good day, sir."

He began to close the door in his face, but Dupont stopped him.

"It's not like that. Okay, just think about it."

When he left, I sank onto the sofa, rubbing my forehead in exhaustion. Bennett leaned into me and twisted one of my locks around his finger.

"What just happened?"

"I'm too tired for this," I muttered, putting a pillow under my head. "Let's just forget everything we just heard and sleep until it's dark. Then we can focus on this whole 'secret room' thing in peace, okay?"

"Okay. But promise me you won't listen to him. I couldn't bear it," Bennett whispered, his lips inches from mine, "promise you won't join the Resistance."

"I promise. The excitement of your companionship is enough adventure for me."

14

Chapter Fourteen

I leaned against the wall opposite Bennett, toying with his stethoscope in my hands.

"Maybe he's not coming," I whispered gently in French as we waited together in the doctor's office.

"It's been two and a half weeks." Ben grumbled, lying down on the examination table with his hands behind his head, moaning, "He better come. He had better arrive. I haven't slept in days, trying to build that fake wall so he has a safe place to stay. If he doesn't show up, I suppose I'll have to pull someone in from the street so at least someone can benefit from my efforts."

I smiled and nestled next to him on the table, gazing up at the water-stained ceiling above us. Since Gerard Dupont's previous visit, we had been working tirelessly to prepare for the arrival of our first Resistance refugee. In addition to constructing a concealed panel behind the guest bedroom, we began to build relationships with the neighbors and others in the region, and several had already scheduled medical appointments with Bennett. Things were going well.

The front door creaked open, and I peered out of the rear examination room to see who was there. I glanced back at Ben, disappointed.

"C'est une femme. It is a lady."

He groaned, sat up in resignation, and fixed his hair before greeting her outside. I remained in the back, listening absentmindedly. Wednesdays were usually calm in Old Marseilles, especially when we were expecting a guest.

"How can I help you, Madame?" he spoke warmly.

"I've been feeling poorly lately; my ear is throbbing horribly, and I fear I've just fractured my thumb. Imagine that! How clumsy can I be?"

I sat up, surprised, and Bennett's silence revealed his uncertainty as well. Standing in the darkness of the examination room, I watched the situation unfold. Dupont had certainly not suggested that we should expect a woman, but she had mentioned the exact two symptoms we had been trained to watch for.

"Well," Bennett stuttered, "I think we should be able to assist you with that. Please give me your name, and I'll bring you back in a minute."

"Merci," she murmured shakily, glancing back and briefly making eye contact with me.

"I am Madame Andrée. I don't mind waiting."

I couldn't keep the grin from spreading across my face.

When she sat down, Ben turned and made a beeline toward me, his expression filled with alarm. I giggled slightly as he grasped my hands in his and murmured, "What do we do?"

"Bring her in here!" I was about to turn to uncover the concealed stairway that led to the hiding area above when Bennett grabbed my arm.

"How do you know this isn't a trick? Dupont never mentioned a woman."

I smiled. "Don't you know who that is? That's Norma Wells. The White Mole. There's a five-million-franc reward on her head. That's our Resistance member, dear; I've never been more certain of anything."

Bennett lifted his eyebrows and glanced back at the thin, dark-haired Frenchwoman sitting impatiently in the waiting area.

"Are you sure?"

"Yes. I'll go get her."

He seemed to yield, taking up the task of removing the furniture that was blocking the fake wall as I headed to the front of the office.

"Madame Andrée? I'm Louise Girard, your doctor's wife. Could I accompany you back?"

She stared at me, picked up her purse, and muttered, "Madame Sterling. I've heard a lot about you, my darling."

She recognized me. She followed me into the small stairwell inside the examination room wall panel, with Bennett trailing after us.

When we were safely inside the guest chamber upstairs, Bennett shook her hand and said, "Miss Wells. I assume you're the one who will be staying with us for a few days. My wife seems to know you, although I don't believe we've met."

She smiled slightly and glanced at me. "We female warriors need to stick together, Monsieur Sterling. Her exploits are well known among the Resistance."

My heart leaped with delight at her compliments. Knowing that people were aware of and concerned about my loneliness, injuries, and blunders as an agent gave me hope that what I was doing was worthwhile.

"And," she said, "I won't be staying for three days; I have to leave in the morning. The Gestapo found me sooner than we expected. Your hospitality, though, is still fantastic."

Bennett excused himself to return to work downstairs, while Norma and I went to the kitchen to get something to eat. With two cups of rationed coffee substitute in front of us, I looked her in the eye. She was putting on a brave front, but she seemed upset.

"Qu'est-ce qui ne va pas? What's wrong?" I inquired.

A tear slid down her cheek, and she moaned. "I don't want to leave Marseilles. They're going after my husband, Harold, and I didn't even get to say goodbye. I never thought..." she paused in pain, "that it would be this hard."

I pulled her into my arms and let her cry freely. I knew exactly how she felt; the agony of not knowing what to do next when everything had been taken away was all too familiar to me.

"I'm sorry," she said in French, "for coming into your welcoming home like a wet blanket."

Holding out a hand, I quietly answered, "Don't be sorry, sweetheart. Cry all you want."

We sipped our coffee in comfortable silence, both grateful to be in the company of someone who understood the ups and downs of our work. About an hour later, Bennett walked in from downstairs in his white coat, hands full of pharmaceutical bottles, chatting about some patient who wouldn't answer any of his questions properly while pouring himself a drink of water. When he noticed our expressions, he stopped speaking and bit his lip.

"Am I interrupting something?" he asked quietly in French.

"No, but you should probably get back downstairs anyway. I love you, darling."

He raised his eyebrow and left awkwardly, the sound of him drinking from his glass echoing all the way down the stairs.

After he left, we laughed at the encounter.

"You two are perfect for each other," she said, smiling. "You can just feel the chemistry between you when you're together."

I smiled shyly. "Thank you. This whole marriage thing," I replied with a grin, "is not as simple as they make it seem. We fight constantly."

"Of course you do. That's how it should be. What kind of relationship would you have if you always agreed with each other and gave in all the time? 'Our marriage is worth fighting for, my love.' That's what my Harold always says."

My heart swelled with contentment. Aside from Bennett, I'd never had someone understand, empathize with, or connect with me the way she did. It was refreshing. That night, we cleared the house of all evidence of her presence, and the three of us sat in our nightclothes by the sputtering heater, listening absentmindedly to Nazi radio broadcasts.

One thin brown piece of paper was placed into the government-issue radio machine, allowing us to listen to BBC, Radio Moscow, Beromünster of Switzerland, and Voice of America. But we could never take the risk, not with Norma's life on the line.

Later in the night, Bennett drew me into his arms as we lay in bed, both of us unable to stop thinking about the fugitive resting just beyond the wall. If the Gestapo knew who she was, they would undoubtedly be tracking her every move, bringing them right to Monsieur Alain Girard, M.D., and his intelligence agent wife, Madame Louise. We would be discovered.

As if my thoughts had conjured it, there was a loud bang on the door. My heart stopped, and I could feel Bennett's hands around my waist and shoulders grow colder. I imagined Norma sitting up in the small cot we had carried into the hiding spot, clutching the quilt with both hands. Ben crawled out from beneath the blankets and muttered, "Stay in bed. I'll tell them you've had a fever and a toothache, okay? If they come in, act irritated that they're disturbing us. Stay calm."

I nodded, and he kissed me gently on the forehead before rushing out into the sitting room, throwing on his robe.

"Are you Herr Alain Girard?" someone at the door asked in a thick German accent. Bennett cleared his throat, and I assumed he nodded in agreement.

"We're looking for this woman; have you seen her?"

My heart sank. The best-case scenario was that they were showing Norma's picture to everyone in our neighborhood, and we were just one of many people asked to identify her. The worst-case scenario was that they already knew she was in our house and were trying to catch Ben in a lie.

Ben, of course, played along, adding, "Well, I can't say she looks familiar, but I'm not very good at remembering faces, sir. Where would I know her from?"

My hands were shaking. I could almost sense Norma's terror from her hiding spot. Perhaps it was just my own.

"She's a fugitive, Herr Girard. We believe she's working for the enemy as a courier."

"Oh my! I can't remember her face, but I'll keep an eye out for her!" Bennett replied cheerfully.

"Do you live alone?" I furrowed my brow at the unexpected question, but Bennett responded calmly.

"No, sir. My wife is in the next room and isn't feeling well. You know how the cold weather affects the ladies."

They mumbled in agreement, and one said, "Are you going to take her to the doctor?"

"Oh, well, I'm a doctor," Bennett said, "and I own the office below. I hope it's just a cold, but I'll give her something tomorrow."

"Good," one of them said. "Perhaps we'll visit your office sometime; it's so hard to find good French doctors."

I was eager to get them out of our home, but Bennett was clearly more opportunistic. Nazi patients would undoubtedly be an easy source of information.

"Oh, you definitely should! My wife speaks better German than I do, but I take pride in being a quick learner. You can expect the same level of service as you would in Berlin or Kaufbeuren."

"Where are you two from?" Even though I knew Ben was trying to build rapport and keep their guard down, every second the conversation lasted added to my anxiety. Norma was undoubtedly frightened.

"I live in Frankfurt, but I was born in Vienna."

"Herrsching," the other one said, "is a small town." I stiffened. That was the location of the safe house where I had been attacked before being captured and sent to England. I touched the scar on my neck where a bullet had grazed me, wondering if he knew who had shot me.

"Wonderful!" Bennett exclaimed, seemingly wrapping up the conversation. "Well, I hope to see you two again soon, and good luck with the search!"

When I heard the door shut, Bennett ran back into our room, his eyebrows raised. Just as he was about to speak, I leapt out of bed and placed my hand over his lips.

"Check for listening devices," I whispered, pulling on a robe over my nightgown and following him into the living room.

We went through the procedure we'd performed so many times in training. Every time someone entered our home, we had to do the same sweep. When we were certain there were no bugs, I led Bennett into the guest bedroom next to ours. I removed all the books from the lowest two shelves of our bookshelf, revealing the small door that led to Norma's hiding spot.

"You first," I said, "I'm in my nightgown."

Bennett started sliding through the door.

"We're married, darling."

"I know," I grinned, "but it's still indecent."

He laughed and helped me through. Bennett rounded the corner to where Norma was sleeping first, whispering, "You're never going to believe this, Louella."

"What?" I gasped as I caught up to where he was standing. Norma had slept soundly through it all, her hair curled like mine, with the blankets wrapped snugly around her face.

"And I was afraid she would worry herself to death back here," I said with a chuckle. "Let's not wake her; she has a long walk ahead of her tomorrow."

We crawled back into bed silently, and Bennett drew me into his arms.

"Why are you shaking?" he asked softly, grasping my hand.

I raised my eyebrows. "How are you not shaking after what just happened?"

He shrugged and let out a faint yawn, tugging on one of my hair's metal curlers. "I don't know; maybe I haven't seen as much as you have. It doesn't scare me as much."

Bennett was right. The thought of being discovered terrified me. I couldn't help but recall the night I was attacked in my Munich flat or the awful sensation of seeing Herr Giroux dead on his kitchen floor in Herrsching.

Despite my experience in espionage, I was not one for confrontation. I preferred working in the shadows, hiding just long enough to escape before the enemies noticed me. Any deviation from that approach filled me with dread.

"Well, if you aren't thinking about being caught, what are you thinking about right now?" I asked Bennett, who was staring up at the ceiling.

"I miss my leather jackets."

15

Chapter Fifteen

The following morning, Norma departed before the sun rose. The three of us ate a little breakfast together under the light of one weak candle (so as not to draw attention to ourselves), while Norma instructed us on how to route our future guests across the Pyrenees. She collected her tiny bag of stuff and exited via our back door, gratefully thanking us for our generosity. We all agreed that, although last night went smoothly, we needed a way to inform our guests when it was unsafe for them to leave the hiding place—just in case.

The following day, Bennett built a buzzer system throughout the property, including one downstairs at the reception desk and one in each of his exam rooms. It was merely a faint hum, something only those who were familiar with the sound could detect, yet it was enough to provide us with an extra degree of protection.

The next few months were a blur of activity for us, as we took in any refugees or Jews that Dupont decided to send our way, corresponded with the OSS about everything from Nazi morale to the distances between certain streets in the city, and tried to blend in as regular French citizens.

One day, while returning from the hairdresser, someone grabbed my elbow and dragged me behind one of the market booths along the street. I yanked my hand away and elbowed the guy hard in the chest, forcing him to lose his grasp on me and collapse in agony. I was about to flee when a guy cried out, "Lux et Veritas, Madame Girard." That was Yale University's Latin motto, and it served as our signal word for the OSS anytime they wanted to contact us. We were meant to trust anybody who knew the term.

"Qui es-tu?" I inquired tersely. "Who are you?" He rose up, groaning, and felt the spot on his chest where I had struck him. "Are you Louise Girard?" he inquired, dodging the question with weak French. I was perplexed. He certainly wasn't with the OSS since he didn't seem to know my true name, but he didn't speak French well. I surmised from his accent that he spoke English, but I wasn't willing to let my guard down too much.

"You did not respond to me. Who are you?"

"Listen," the guy said in English before catching himself. "Écoute. I need your aid. You need to...follow me." I sneered and rolled my eyes at him. "No," I said. "How about you follow me?" I started going towards an alley I knew would be vacant, and in desperation, he followed close behind. I wasn't even sure if he comprehended what I had just said since I talked rapidly and in the most colloquial French I knew to make him feel uncomfortable. This was clearly not going as smoothly as he had anticipated. Once in the deserted lane, I abandoned the French.

"Who are you?" He responded honestly because he was taken aback by my flawless English. "First Lieutenant Carter, Eighth Fleet, United States Air Force. I was supposed to locate you. Who are you? Why are you here in France?"

"It doesn't matter; you can call me Louise Girard. Did you crash anywhere?"

"There are twenty of us. It was a transport operation, basically trying to get everyone to Normandy, but there was a bird attack. Imagine being pushed out of the skies by birds when there are anti-aircraft missiles all around! As an afterthought," he remarked, "When birds get into the-"

"I know what a bird strike is."

"Just making sure."

I exhaled. "Is anyone hurt? Who instructed you to come see me?"

"Minor injuries only. Someone from the Resistance...named Gerard, I believe. He caught us disposing of our uniforms and almost shot us. He stated we were glad it was him and not someone else, and he told us to send someone to Marseille to locate you. I thought of Gerard Dupont. The arrogant communist had allegedly resorted to helping lost Americans."

"Alright," I said, jotting my address on a tiny paper, "bring them here. As long as you agree that they will behave and stay quiet, you will all have a place to sleep—though I cannot guarantee a bed." He smiled. "Thank you. Oh, how pleased I am to be able to tell them all good news. Thank you, ma'am. You won't even realize we're there."

"Well, I surely know that won't be true," I answered with a tiny grin. "Our home will be so crowded that there won't even be space to stand. Listen, no more than two people should be allowed to enter the city at once. At least thirty minutes apart, and preferably more. There are no uniforms, no English, no covert looks, winks, or efforts at secret codes. I'm sure you're one of the few who knows any French."

He nodded and shrugged slightly. "The Captain is rather proficient, but he is the only one. I would not even call what I know 'speaking French.'"

"Alright. Silence will serve as a signal for me to identify you all. Approach the desk but don't talk. I'll know. If your Captain isn't already planning on coming last, ask him to do so. For the sake of both parties' safety, we will stage all of you in one of the rear examination rooms until you are all present, at which point we will transport you all upstairs. There can be no sound coming from that room, so bring some playing cards."

I leaned against the brick alley wall and placed a palm on my brow. Dupont would hear it from me later. Volunteering Bennett and myself to take on 20 American soldiers? We could barely manage a Jewish family of three at this stage.

"Don't tell anybody that I am not French, or even my name. Perhaps I'll inform your Captain after everyone is securely inside the home, but I can't risk your capture."

He nodded. "I will see you soon, Ma'am. I cannot thank you enough."

"Thank you for not putting my family and future possibilities to serve others at jeopardy. See you soon, First Lieutenant Carter."

I hastily exited the lane, straying as far away from the location as possible before considering going back.

As I ran into the waiting area, a bell above the door jingled, and Bennett wrinkled his brow as we made eye contact. He got up from where he had his feet up on the desk, perhaps seeing the sorrow in my gaze.

I turned the 'open' sign in the window to 'closed,' and signaled with my finger for him to join me upstairs. "Do you have any other appointments today?"

"Just one, but I'll cancel-"

"Don't," I urged. "This would be too evident. Just come upstairs."

He followed me up the ornately decorated wood staircase and seized my hands in his as soon as we were in the kitchen.

"What's wrong? Are we in danger?"

"We're going to have twenty American airmen living with us, Ben. Can you collect all of the blankets, pillows, and mattresses we have? I'll work from the desk downstairs."

Bennett shook his head, disbelieving. "Why are they in Marseille? How could they know?"

"It seems that Dupont told them. They're arriving in groups of two, roughly 30 minutes apart. Their aircraft crashed following a bird attack, and they need somewhere to stay." I stopped for a second before adding, "It was a transportation mission."

He glanced up at me tentatively. We were on a delivery mission when my female crew crashed in the French countryside in 1941. Bennett understood that I felt driven to assist these guys.

"Okay, we can probably squeeze eight or nine people in the hiding area to sleep, and the remainder can stay in the guest room on the floor. If there is a danger or someone calls, they will all have to squeeze into the hiding location together for a time. Ring for me if my four o'clock appointment arrives."

I agreed and raced down the stairs, sitting tensely in the chair behind Ben's desk, trying to keep myself occupied.

Sure enough, the four o'clock appointment arrived exactly on time, and I hastily summoned Bennett down, urgently praying that the first of the American troops would not come in right then.

When Bennett and his patient were safely inside the exam room farthest from the concealed stairs, I relaxed somewhat and kept a tight eye on the door. A few minutes later, two tall, blond guys in white undershirts and ill-fitting pants entered, staring at me worriedly.

They approached the counter but said nothing, seeming uncertain of themselves. I nodded quietly and beckoned for them to follow me into the rear examination room, which led to the stairwell.

"Be comfortable; don't say anything. Do you have something to keep yourself occupied?"

One of them proudly took out a deck of playing cards from his pocket. I grinned.

After locking the door behind them, I returned to my seat at Bennett's desk. I sat on my shaking hands, trying to seem cool in case someone entered.

The American flyboys entered the examination room stealthily, two by two, with Bennett leading them while I prepared upstairs. When they had all been found and darkness had fallen, Ben opened the short stairway and rushed up to me.

"Lou?" he said. "There are twenty of them. Are we ready?"

"Relatively. I'll bring them up, and you show them where they'll be staying." I couldn't help but shake as I beckoned for the guys to come up the steps.

"Come on, boys," I said in English with a French accent. "My husband will show you where to go."

Each one passed, and I slapped them on the back, their tired, strained faces relaxing at the fragrance of rationed eggs. I nodded to First Lieutenant Carter as he passed, and he grinned. One of them was clutching his nose as blood poured down his chin, so I extended my hand to move him away.

"You'll need to clean it up, and I'll meet you in the kitchen. Do not bleed on my floor."

"Yes, Ma'am."

"Captain," I told the final guy in line, "I'm glad to see that you've all made it." The guy appeared astonished when he saw me.

"I didn't expect you to know my rank; is that something they teach to ladies here in Marseille?" I smiled pleasantly.

"I'm a Colonel with the Women's Army Service Pilots. So now I'm acting as an agent. I am with the OSS." He raised his eyebrows and took a step back.

"Oh. Forgive me, Ma'am; I suppose you were higher in status at the time. I didn't know you were American."

I grinned as I lowered my voice and dropped the accent. "That is the hope. You may call me Louise, but do not tell your guys anything. I am simply a Frenchwoman who wants to do her bit, okay?"

"Yes, ma'am. Thank you so much for your assistance...I thought I'd lose all of my men."

"I understand the sensation. You'll be secure here; just make sure they're quiet tonight." I proceeded to the kitchen, where the guy with a bleeding nose was sitting on the floor, trying in vain not to spill blood on the floor. "Alright, come on up and sit here," I replied, pulling out a chair for him, "don't worry about the floor. It's easy to clean." I removed his hand and cleaned his face with a dishrag. "It's definitely broken," I said. "What's your name?"

"Chester."

"And how did you come out with an injury and everyone else seems to have escaped unhurt?"

He shrugged. "The birds struck the aircraft, and we were instantly in free fall. Ma'am, this isn't what they usually tell happens when the engines fail. I didn't sit down like the rest of them, so I believe I flew all over the place. I can't remember." Chester paused, as if overtaken with emotion. "I believed I was already dead. So now I'm alive? It's very—I don't know—scary."

I held his hand and looked him in the eyes, compassionately. "I am quite familiar with the emotion. Everyone pats you on the back and tells you you're a hero, that you must be courageous and focus on triumph, but all you can think about is how much you miss the way things were before you became a hero."

He grinned slightly. "That is precisely it. You talk as if you've seen war, Ma'am."

I shrugged sheepishly, relaxed enough to let my guard down a bit. "You boys have more allies than you know...stationed all over the world."

Chester cast me a sideways look, thinking, "You're an American, aren't you?"

"I guess you'll never know." We both knew.

"I've got a girl back home named Diana. Do you suppose I could borrow paper and a pen to write to her? I promised her I'd marry her as soon as I came back."

"Of course," I said, "I'm sure she's a doll." Chester was beaming with delight as I departed to fetch him a pen. The sound of breaking glass caused me to turn in the other direction, where I saw two of the guys busily cleaning up the shattered pieces of a vase in the corridor.

"I'm really sorry, Ma'am. I'm sorry, but we didn't notice it."

I raised my hand and started assisting them in cleaning up the fragments.

"It's fine. Don't worry about it; I have no idea where this vase came from."

They proceeded to apologize profusely as we disposed of the pieces in the trash can, and Bennett arrived to assist in leading them and the rest of the guys into the bedroom and hiding spot to prepare for the evening.

I softly excused myself, breathing deeply, and leaned against the wall in our own bedroom, unable to hold back the tears.

"Louise?" Bennett said in a cautious voice as he rushed in and closed the door behind him, "What's wrong?"

"They broke the vase," I wailed quietly, folding my hands and placing them on my forehead.

Ben wrapped his arm around me and drew me to his chest. "What's really wrong?"

I halted for a time, tears falling on my knees. "I wish I hadn't lied about my age on the enrollment paperwork. Why would I do something like that? I wrote that I was twenty-one, the legal minimum age for women in Britain at the time, despite the fact that I was only nineteen."

He wrinkled his brow and placed a delicate hand on my cheek, brushing away tears with his thumb as he calmly said, "You mean back when you enrolled in England? That was 1940, sweetie, and you're too good at your job to be called out on it today. That would be the Allied troops' worst miscalculation. Again, I don't believe that is your issue."

I exhaled. "I do not know, Alain. Everything is terrible, hard, and dangerous right now. Should I start with the fact that I can't even address you by your true name in the privacy of our own room? I cannot stop—" My breathing grew shallow as I fought not to cry. "I can't stop thinking about the aircraft accident. Every time I close my eyes, I see it." I let him take my hand as we sat on the floor with our backs to the sage green wallpaper.

Given how much I'd buried my sentiments over the tragedy in 1941, Bennett seemed surprised by how much it impacted me. Perhaps I didn't really comprehend that until now.

"What can I do to help?"

"I don't know."

"Okay. We can just sit together."

"Thank you."

He tenderly kissed my forehead.

To be continued....

Author Note

I'm thrilled to share with you my book, and let me tell you, the journey to bring it to life has been nothing short of exhilarating. Pouring my heart and soul into these pages, this book has been a labor of love, and I've worked tirelessly to ensure that every word, every twist, and every turn captivates your imagination and takes you on an unforgettable adventure.

I'm eager to hear your thoughts and feedback. They mean the world to me, not only because they validate the countless hours of dedication I've put into this work but also because they provide invaluable insights that will help me improve and grow as a writer.

About the Author

Emily Higgs is a vibrant voice in the realm of fiction, weaving intricate tales that transport readers to captivating worlds. With a pen dipped in imagination and a mind brimming with creativity, she effortlessly spins narratives that enthrall and enchant.

Born with a passion for storytelling, Emily's journey as a writer began at a young age when she would pen short stories and poems, each one a glimpse into her boundless imagination. As she grew, so did her love for the written word, and she soon found herself immersed in the art of crafting novels.